LESSON 1:

Glues, fillers, and eliminating seams

Better-looking models start with the basics

BY PAUL BOYER

ALL RIGHT, CLASS, get comfortable. Find a good seat — an easy chair is fine, but the stool at your workbench is even better. This is a lab course, and I'll assume you all have the basic supplies on hand — a kit you're itching to build, basic modeling tools, and above-average interest in this hobby. All set? Let's go.

What separates a poor model from a good one? Anyone? Right. Blobs of glue, gaping seams, streaky paint, upside-down markings, and broken and missing parts are telltale signs of a disappointing model. Yes, we've all made models that look like that, so how do we improve? Discovering new skills isn't enough; you have to practice them. The more you practice, the more natural these skills will seem, and the more comfortable you become building models, the more you'll enjoy the hobby.

Glues. Since most of the models we build are plastic, we'll discuss plastic solvent cements first. The two types are liquid and "tube" cements, Fig. 1. Both work on the same principle; they dissolve the plastic at the mating surface, and when set, create a bond by welding the pieces together. Liquids are usually applied while holding the pieces together. A small quantity applied to the seam between the parts runs along the seam by capillary action. Holding the parts together while the solvent action takes place ensures a good bond.

Tube glue is liquid solvent cement with a polymer added to give it body and make it easier to apply. Tube glue takes longer to set and is applied to the mating surface of one of the parts, then the parts are joined.

Let's go back to one of those badly built models, where someone committed half a tube of glue to the premise that more is better. "That part won't stay on . . . use *more* glue!" Little did this fellow realize that glue isn't stickum. He's reinforced chronically broken parts and bridged gaps between poorly fitting parts with tube glue. Excess glue will only melt and distort the plastic, ruining the model. Tube glue should never be used as a filler — we'll discuss what you should use later in this lesson.

Epoxy is a two-part adhesive which can bond almost anything and works best for mating dissimilar materials such as metal to wood, plastic to metal, and so forth. Equal amounts of the two parts are mixed, starting a chemical reaction that cures the glue in as little as five minutes.

Super glues (cyanoacrylates) also are good at bonding dissimilar materials, and they set up instantly. Slow-setting, gap-filling, and gel super glues work well as fillers (more on that later).

White glue (polyvinyl acetate) such as Elmer's Glue-All is good for bonding porous materials such as wood and paper. We'll also use white glue to attach small parts where bond strength isn't important. Since white glue dries clear, it is best for attaching clear plastic parts such as headlights, canopies, and windshields, Fig. 2.

Fillers, including the teacher's pet. You may be asking, "what is a filler and why do I need it?" First, why? To

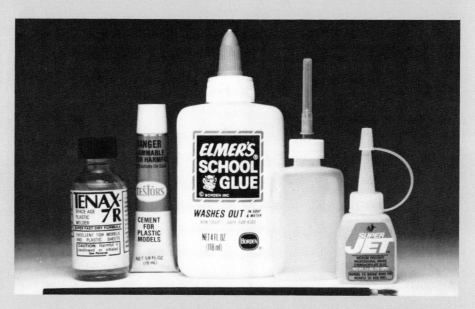

Fig. 1. Solvent cements weld plastic joints with a chemical bond. Liquid cements can be applied with a brush or applicator bottle (shown with protective cap over the needle). Super glue can also be used and has valuable properties as a filler. A bottle of white glue also should be on your workbench.

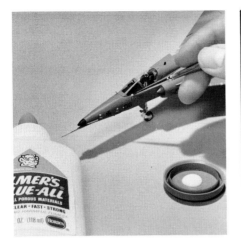

Fig. 2. White glue is the best cement to attach clear parts — it dries clear, doesn't craze (etch) plastic, and fills the seams around the parts.

Fig. 3. Gap-filling super glue used with an accelerator will become your favorite filler, once you get used to it. There are many brands of super glue, each with its own accelerator, but they can be used interchangeably.

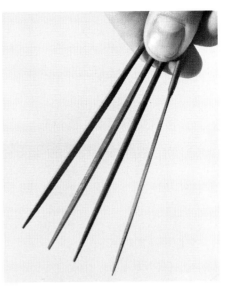

Fig. 4. You'll need small modeling files. Half-round, round, flat, square, and triangular files come in handy for adjusting poor-fitting parts.

mold plastic kits, manufacturers must divide the model into parts. When we build the model, we reverse the process, but the seams between the parts are often visible. Sometimes that's okay, but in most cases, the seams are ugly — they should be eliminated to produce a realistic replica.

The best way to eliminate seams is to improve poor-fitting joints. When that fails, the gaps can be hidden with filler. A filler is a soft, pliable substance that can be poured or pushed into gaps and surface imperfections. After the filler sets, excess material is sanded away, leveling the surface and concealing the gaps and sinkholes (depressions caused by insufficient plastic in moldings).

Many different fillers are available, including auto body fillers, epoxy putty, and even spackling paste. But my favorite is gap-filling super glue used with accelerator, Fig. 3.

As with any filler, there is good news and bad news about super glue. The bad news is that (if improperly used) it bonds skin together instantly. Also, some people experience eye, nose, and throat irritation from the fumes. I've never had problems, but I know modelers who refuse to use super glue because of this.

There's no arguing about the usefulness of super glues, though. I use them with a spray accelerator. Apply a little super glue to a seam or sinkhole, spray on accelerator, and the glue sets in seconds. More applications of glue and accelerator fill the imperfections, and you're ready to sand.

Super glue bonds to the surface of just about any material. Cured super glue is slightly harder than styrene but can be sanded easily, and, best of all, you only have to wait about a minute before sanding. Large amounts of super glue will shrink slightly when setting, but you'll be able to determine the de-

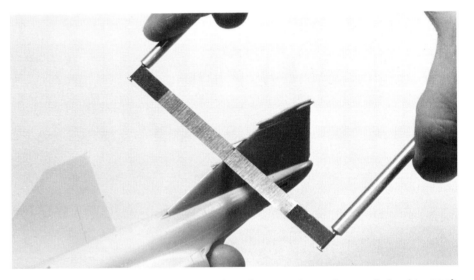

Fig. 5. The "Flexi-file" is a handy gadget that allows you to sand seams in hard-to-reach spots, such as between these two delicate pitot tubes.

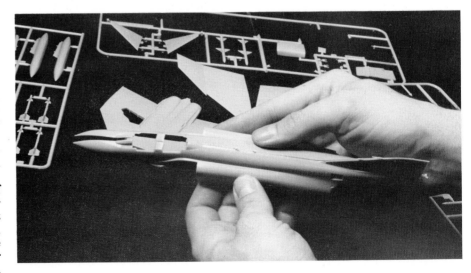

Fig. 6. Dry-fitting parts will help you discover potential fit problems.

Fig. 7. Parts fit better if you lightly sand the mating surfaces.

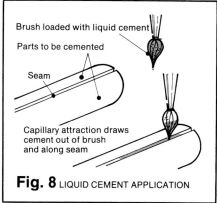

Brush loaded with liquid cement

Parts to be cemented

Seam

Capillary attraction draws cement out of brush and along seam

Fig. 8 LIQUID CEMENT APPLICATION

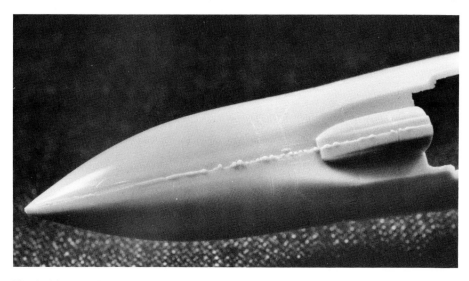

Fig. 9. After waiting a few seconds, the liquid cement will soften the plastic. Then you can press the parts together, and softened plastic will ooze out of the seam.

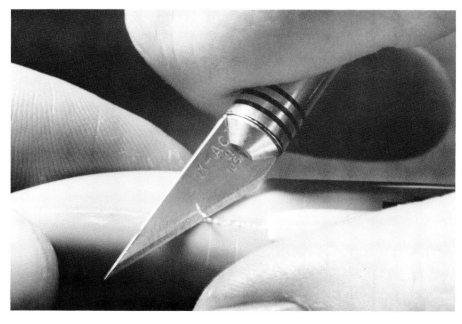

Fig. 10. After the joint is set, shave and sand away the excess plastic.

gree of shrinkage right away and add more to correct it. Unlike other fillers, you can fill, sand, prime, inspect, fill, and sand again all in one modeling session — no more waiting a few days for filler to dry.

Tools of the trade. Modeling files, Fig. 4, are a good investment, and are available in most hobby shops. Sandpaper is a necessity and is inexpensive — my favorites are 220-, 320-, 400-, and 600-grit wet-or-dry sandpaper, available in any hardware store.

Another handy gadget is the Flexi-file (Creations Unlimited, 2929 Montreat Drive, N. E., Grand Rapids, MI 49505). It's an aluminum tube handle that holds a thin strip of abrasive-coated Mylar film, Fig. 5. The Flexi-file can get into places you can't reach with your fingers or a sanding block.

Learning by doing. Now let's apply what we've learned. I'll assume you know how to build kits, how to remove parts from plastic sprues, how to clean up mold marks, and so forth. Start by dry-fitting parts to look for potential fit problems, Fig. 6. Remember, the better the fit, the less filling and sanding you'll have to do. Sometimes you'll have to remove those handy little alignment pins to improve the fit. Sanding the mating surfaces is also a good idea as it eliminates uneven edges, Fig. 7.

One of the easiest ways to produce gapless seams is the "squeeze method." This takes advantage of the effect of solvent cements on plastic. First, hold the parts together loosely. Apply liquid solvent with a brush, ruling pen, or applicator bottle — just a drop. Simply touching the applicator to the seam will cause the liquid to run down the seam, Fig. 8. Wait a few seconds for the solvent to soften the plastic on both sides of the seam. Now squeeze the parts together. Note how the softened plastic oozes out of the seam, Fig. 9. This extra plastic acts as a filler. Don't repeatedly squeeze and release as this draws air into the softened plastic and creates tiny bubbles that will have to be filled later.

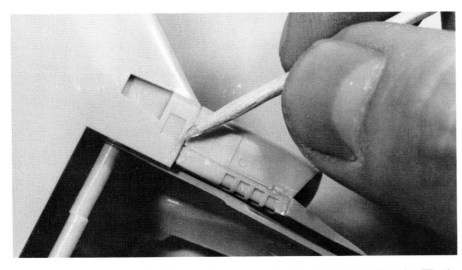

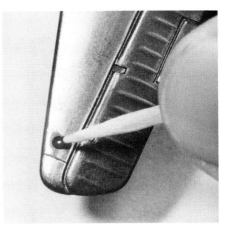

Fig. 11. The "squeeze method" doesn't always work. Your instructor's favorite filler is gap-filling super glue. A small amount of the glue is applied with a toothpick and allowed to flow into the seam.

Fig. 13. Super glue can also fill those annoying ejector pin marks.

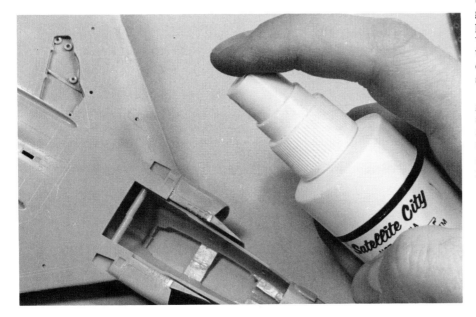

Fig. 12. Once the super glue has settled where you want it, set it by spraying on an accelerator. Super glue will set in seconds.

After allowing the assembly to dry for a day, remove the excess plastic with a sharp hobby knife, files, and sandpaper, Fig. 10. Scrub out sanding residue with an old toothbrush and inspect the seams for voids and depressions.

Not every seam will be perfectly filled with the squeeze method, and that's where fillers come in. Deposit a large drop of gap-filling super glue on a swatch of scrap sheet styrene. Dip a toothpick into the super glue and transfer it to the seam, Fig. 11. Touch the toothpick to the seam and watch the super glue flow into the depression. You can also prod the glue along the seam with the toothpick.

Now observe the glue as it settles into the gap. You can move the glue around with the toothpick or by tilting

the assembly so gravity pulls the glue down the seam. Once you have the glue where you want it, spray on accelerator, Fig. 12. Within seconds, the super glue sets. Check to see if you'll need more to fill the void, then repeat the process until all seams are filled.

Super glue is also good for leveling off those curious circular depressions you see in some plastic kits (these are created by ejector pins in the injection-molding machines). Simply apply a tiny drop to the center of the depression, allow the glue to flow and fill the depression, then spray on accelerator, Fig. 13.

Filing and sanding. No matter which filler you use, you'll likely have to do a little filing and sanding to level the filler with the surface of the model. Start by removing as much material

with the files as you can. If you look closely, you'll see that the files leave tiny cut marks. Next, sand with 400-grit sandpaper and water. Water helps prevent the sandpaper from clogging with residue and speeds its cutting action. Sand in small circles where you can. Wipe away the slurry, then finish sanding with 600-grit sandpaper.

Sanding with successively finer grades of sandpaper eliminates the scratches from the previous paper's abrasive grit. A good wet sanding with 600-grit paper is the final cleanup stage before our next lesson — preparing for painting. See you then! **FSM**

END LESSON 1

HOMEWORK ASSIGNMENT 1

Practice, practice, practice

Materials: Plastic model kit, liquid solvent cement, gap-filling super glue, super glue accelerator

Tools: Cement applicator (brush or syringe), sharp hobby knife, small files, 320-, 400-, 600-grit wet-or-dry sandpaper

☐ Reread this lesson.
☐ Open the kit box and examine the instructions carefully. Cut the parts from the sprues and clean up flash and mold marks. Dry-fit the major parts, but leave the small parts on the sprues until needed.
☐ Lightly sand all mating surfaces.
☐ If parts fit poorly, file and sand to achieve the best fit possible.
☐ Following the order on the instruction sheet, assemble the model with liquid solvent cement. Use the "squeeze method" to fill the joints.
☐ After waiting one day, fill remaining gaps and surface imperfections with gap-filling super glue and accelerator.
☐ File and sand excess filler smooth.

AFTER SCHOOL

Now I'll take questions about Lesson 1, glues, fillers, and eliminating seams. Yes sir?

"Jim Ireland, Sacramento, California. I've found super glues to be best for filling small areas, but for large ones I prefer auto body filler. It seems the super glue is much harder than plastic, requiring vigorous sanding that can eliminate surrounding surface detail. Also, it's difficult to create subtle shapes since you have to use so much force to sand super glue. I find it easier to scribe panel lines into putty than in super glue, too."

I'll go along with that, but you should file and sand super glue fillets as soon as they are set. Cured super glue becomes harder after an hour or so. Since the beauty of filling with super glue is speed, you should sand right away. True, auto body fillers are easier to shape, but large shapes must be built up in layers, allowing each to dry before applying the next. My experience with scribing new panel lines is that auto body fillers chip along the scribed line, creating ragged edges. Each of you will have to decide whether time or effort is more important, but I'll stick with super glue.

"Patrick Hoff, Silver Spring, Maryland. Satellite City's UFO thick-formula super glue is claimed not to fog and the fumes won't cause eye and throat irritation. What have you found?"

I tested UFO thick formula on a scrap of clear styrene, placed the scrap in a plastic film can, sprayed on an accelerator, and closed the lid. I repeated the process with Carl Goldberg Models' Super Jet. After waiting a minute, I removed the scraps and, sure enough, the UFO thick didn't fog the clear plastic. Super Jet did. I've never been bothered by super glue fumes, so I can't comment on UFO's properties. Perhaps some of you out there would share your experiences.

"Jon Bakehouse, Hastings, Iowa. Is it absolutely necessary to use an accelerator with super glue?"

No, but if you don't, large areas will take hours to set. The accelerator starts a chemical reaction at the surface of the glue, causing the molecules to form rigid chains throughout the application. Speed is the advantage, so accelerator is worthwhile.

"Jim Short, Satellite Beach, Florida. I have an old Revell kit and on the box it says to use 'S' type cement since the kit is made of styrene. I don't think they make styrene cement anymore since new kits are polystyrene. Which glue should I use on this kit?"

Your question requires a brief history lesson. Revell used to make a few kits from acetate and had an "A" type cement for them. The "S" type cement was for the styrene kits. In our hobby, styrene is simply an abbreviation for polystyrene and any solvent plastic cement will work on "S" kits. If you run across an old Revell "A" kit, you'll have to use acetone to cement the parts.

"Peter Cappiello, Staten Island, New York. I have trouble gluing large areas with liquid glue — it seems to cure before I can press the entire seam together. What am I doing wrong?"

"David Levis, Mason City, Iowa. I have trouble, too. I can't get the plastic to ooze up through the seam. Am I using the wrong brand of glue?"

First, Peter, you're trying to do too much too quickly. Start by holding the parts together loosely and apply the liquid cement to the seam. If you squeeze the parts together hard, the cement won't penetrate to the bonding surfaces. Allow the cement to flow down the seam an inch or so, wait a few seconds, then squeeze. Move on another couple of inches and repeat. That should fix it.

David, it shouldn't matter which brand you use, but you may not be using enough liquid. You should be able to see the cement flow from your applicator into the seam.

"Buck Pilkenton, Edmonds, Washington. In Fig. 7 [Lesson 1], you show sanding the mating surfaces. You may want to stress 'lightly sand' since if you go too far you'll convert a bump into a gap. Also, remind everyone to use wet-or-dry sandpaper when wet sanding. Regular sandpaper will turn to mush if you get it wet."

Thanks, Buck. You're right on both counts.

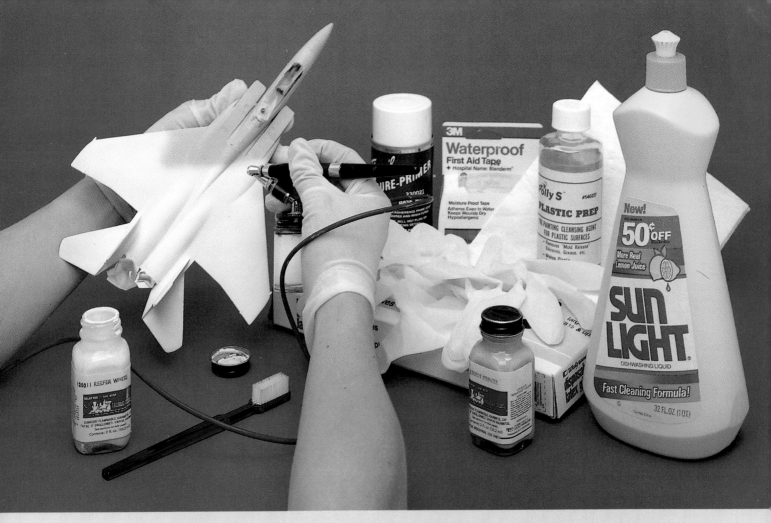

Before the color coats go on, you must prepare the model. Washing and priming will help paint adhesion, while disposable gloves keep skin oils off the plastic.

LESSON 2:

Preparing to paint

An artist always starts with a clean canvas

BY PAUL BOYER

IN OUR FIRST LESSON we covered basic building techniques that eliminated seams and hid fit problems. The next step is to prepare the model for paint.

Why paint? Sure, some kits are molded in the correct color plastic, but few models look good without paint. On top of that, the decal markings included with the kit stick better to paint than to bare plastic. Besides, some of the filling and sanding you did during the first lesson is going to show unless it's covered with paint.

After sanding the seams, filling gaps, and correcting molding flaws, it's time to prepare the surface to accept paint. Styrene plastic kits are usually manufactured by injection molding machines. To ensure the plastic sprues and parts come out of the mold easily, an oily release agent is sprayed into the mold cavity just before injection. Some of this chemical remains on the plastic and can cause painting problems. Oils will prevent most modeling paints from adhering to plastic.

Mold-release agent isn't the only bugaboo. If you munch as you model, the grease and oils from your fries or chocolate bar may be carried to the plastic. You may not be able to see it, but there's even enough natural oil on your skin to affect paint adhesion.

What we're getting down to is that you must wash the model before you paint it. Yep! Scrubbing with good, old-fashioned soap and water and an old toothbrush does wonders. The bristles of the toothbrush are fine enough to dig fine sanding dust out of recessed panel lines, from in between the raised letters on the hood, from around the engine grille, and from other nooks and crannies. The soap (I use a liquid dishwashing detergent) is strong enough to lift mold-release agent and finger oils.

Now we've got a pretty sudsy model, Fig. 1. Rinse it under the tap, allowing the water to fill interior spaces and flow out every opening, Fig. 2. Since water will prevent paint from adhering, too, dry the model with a soft cloth or towel, Fig. 3, being careful that the fabric doesn't snag and damage sharp corners on the model.

There will still be a few drops of water caught in corners inside the model, and I use two methods for removing it. If your schedule allows, just put the model aside and let it air dry — the water will evaporate in a few days. If you're in a hurry, use a hair dryer set on low heat with maximum air. Blow the air into one opening and watch little beads of water scurry out of the others, Fig. 4.

Safe painting. Now we have a clean, dry model. To prevent further contamination from finger oils, slip on disposable latex rubber examination gloves, Fig. 5, available at any drugstore. I use these whenever I paint or handle the model — they also prevent fingerprints from marring fresh paint. Needless to say, the gloves also protect *you* from harmful chemicals in many modeling paints and thinners. A good investment.

The next step is a quick wipe with Polly S Plastic Prep, Fig. 6, a soapy alcohol mixture that cuts through oils and helps reduce static electricity that can attract dust. Wipe it on with a lint-free cloth or chamois. Plastic Prep evaporates rapidly.

Keeping paint out. Before spraying either primer or paint, mask areas you don't want to be painted. Perhaps you have an already-painted cockpit interior, or you'd rather not have a metalflake red engine under the hood. These areas can be masked with a variety of tapes, liquids, and paper.

One of my favorite masking materials is Blenderm medical tape, found in drugstores. Blenderm is a frosty, high-tack tape that is flexible — nearly rubbery. It's ideal for sealing cockpits and other areas since it can stick into tight corners without lifting, Fig. 7.

Be on the lookout for small openings that lead into the areas you don't want paint to reach. Typical of these is a nose gear strut mounting hole that continues through to the cockpit. Any spray that gets in that hole is bound to ruin the painted interior. Also look for

Fig. 1. Gentle scrubbing with an old toothbrush and liquid dishwashing detergent removes sanding debris from recessed panel lines and eliminates mold-release agents and fingerprints.

Fig. 2. Thoroughly rinse the model inside and out with running water.

Fig. 3. Dry the model with a towel or soft cloth, but beware of snagging and damaging small parts and corners.

9

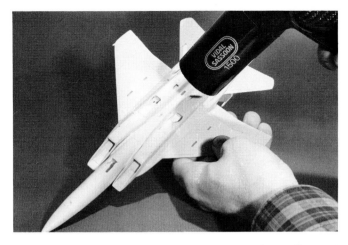

Fig. 4. Force drying interior cavities with a hair dryer will speed things up.

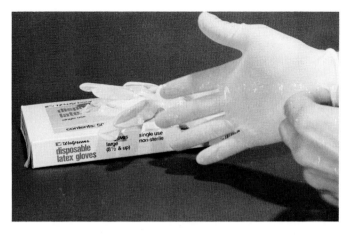

Fig. 5. Disposable latex gloves not only keep oily fingerprints off the model, but help prevent marring fresh paint and help protect you from harmful chemicals.

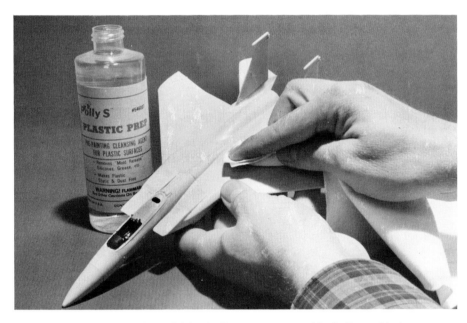

Fig. 6. A final wipe with Polly S Plastic Prep removes residual oils and helps prevent static electricity buildup.

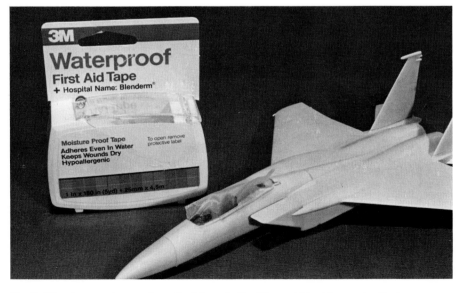

Fig. 7. Blenderm waterproof medical tape is flexible and ideal for protecting areas you don't want painted. Look for it in drugstores.

pylon holes, intakes, exhaust trunks, and other openings.

Do you need a primer? A primer is a white or gray paint applied to the model before the color coats. You can use any white or gray paint, not necessarily one labeled "primer." However, you do want the primer to adhere well to the plastic, have a flat finish, and an ability to highlight surface imperfections.

I don't always prime my models — sometimes it isn't necessary. If I have a good-fitting kit with no putty work and a simple paint scheme, I'll skip the primer. Also, I won't prime if the final finish will be "natural metal." Whether using buffing metallic paints or foil, I need the smoothest, shiniest plastic possible, and primer produces a flat, velvet surface unsuitable for metal finishes. We'll talk more about natural metal finishes in a later lesson.

Another reason to use a primer is with the new acrylic paints. Most acrylic paints are water based and their biggest advantage is that they are nontoxic. The problem is that they don't adhere as well to plastic as paints with more powerful solvents. Sometimes removing masking tape also removes what you thought was a nice, dry paint job! Primers serve as an interface between the paint and the plastic.

I like to airbrush Floquil Primer (120009 or 330009 in the spray can) or white (300011 or 330021 spray can) over the model, Fig. 8. Floquil's paints adhere well to plastic since their lacquer base lightly bites the surface with a solvent chemical reaction. The matte surface of the primer provides "tooth" for the color coats, and that's particularly important for the weak-adhering acrylics.

A primer coat produces a monochromatic surface that makes it easy to spot imperfections. After the primer has set (it usually takes a couple of hours), carefully inspect the model. If seams

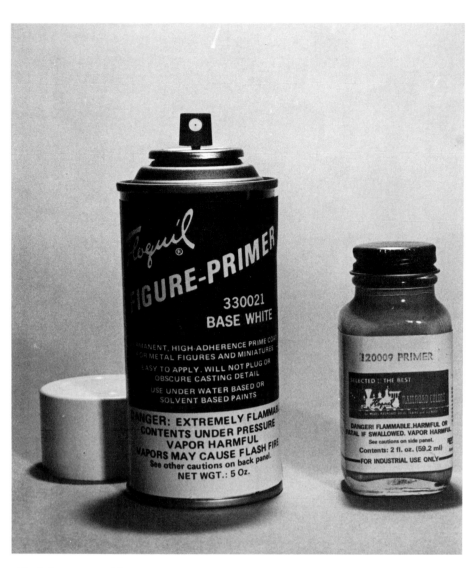

Fig. 8. A spray can of Floquil white figure primer or a bottle of gray primer is an important addition to your paint collection. Primers reveal surface imperfections and help color coats to cover and adhere.

are still showing or high spots or depressions need to be leveled, sand the primer from the offending area, add more super glue filler, set it with accelerator, sand, wash, and reprime. You may have to repeat this process several times to eliminate all imperfections.

In the next lesson, we'll look at the choices of modeling paints and thinners. In the meantime, turn to your homework and practice, practice, practice.

FSM

END LESSON 2

HOMEWORK ASSIGNMENT 2

Clean, prime, sand, and repeat

Materials: Flat white or light gray paint, liquid dishwashing detergent, Blenderm medical tape, Polly S Plastic Prep
Tools: 400- and 600-grit wet-or-dry sandpaper, old toothbrush, chamois, hair dryer, disposable latex gloves

☐ Reread this lesson.
☐ Inspect your model for flaws and sanding scratches left from last lesson.
☐ Using an old toothbrush, wash the entire model with liquid dishwashing detergent and water.
☐ Dry the model with a towel and hair dryer, making sure water trapped inside is blown out.
☐ Wearing disposable latex gloves, use a chamois to wipe Polly S Plastic Prep over the entire model.
☐ Mask areas you want to remain unpainted with Blenderm tape.
☐ Using an airbrush or spray can, prime the model.
☐ Inspect for surface flaws, then correct them with sandpaper.
☐ Prime, inspect, and correct again if necessary.

Modelers have never had it so good — today's choice of paint formulas and colors is wide. Enamels, lacquers, and acrylics are specially formulated for painting plastic models. Most can be hand brushed as well as airbrushed.

FSM'S FINISHING SCHOOL

LESSON 3:

Modeling paints

They're crucial
for a good finish

BY PAUL BOYER

IN OUR SECOND LESSON, we prepared the model for paint. This time, we're going to prepare the *paint* for painting, discuss the different types of paint, when to use each type, and which thinner to use.

Preparing the paint for painting. We all know that paint is used to color an object — that's obvious. But it also seals the surface and hides "body work" — areas of putty or sheet styrene that would otherwise stick out like the proverbial sore thumb.

All paint separates if it sits around

long enough. The heavy pigments settle to the bottom of the container, while the lighter solvent and vehicle rise to the top. Before paint can be used, these elements must be mixed back together to a smooth consistency.

Some modelers carefully stir their paints, saying that shaking them hastens deterioration by mixing air into the paint. I'm not convinced that that is a problem. To thoroughly mix my paint, I drop in a couple of beebees, stir a little with a Popsicle stick, then close the lid and shake the bottle for a couple of minutes, Fig. 1. The beebees act as agitators and help mix the pigment

into the vehicle. I've been using beebees for years and haven't had problems with the metal of the beebees polluting the paint.

Every time you open a paint bottle, a little paint will get on the threads of the cap and bottle. Eventually this will build up and glue the caps to the bottles. Always wipe off the threads with a rag, then carefully screw the cap back onto the bottle.

The quality of the paint can make or break a model. If you have any doubts about a bottle of paint that's been sitting on your shelf for months (or years), don't risk your project — buy a fresh

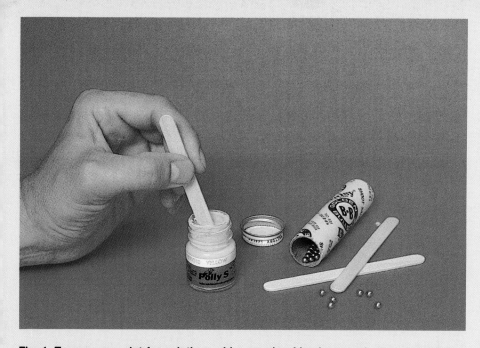

Fig. 1. To prepare paint for painting, add a couple of beebees and stir the heavy pigments up from the bottom of the container. After closing the lid, shake for a minute or two to ensure thorough mixing of the pigment, solvent, and vehicle.

Fig. 2. Enamels, the good old standby, are still available. Most brands now offer specific colors matched to military and automotive standards.

bottle. Don't try to resurrect polluted, separated, half-dried paint; the time you'll waste painting, stripping, and repainting is more valuable than the dollar and a half you'll spend for a fresh bottle.

If you want to save money on paint, think about painting assembly-line fashion. Prepare more than one model for painting with the same color, say, two or three Ferraris (red, of course), or a couple of aircraft with the same camouflage colors.

Model paints today. It used to be that you could purchase a dollar model, a 15-cent tube of glue, and a few 10-cent bottles of paint. Most of us remember the small bottles of glossy Testor and Pactra enamels which came in a rainbow of bright colors. Early in the

1960s, paint manufacturers started paying attention to modelers' pleas for particular colors. Remember Testor, Pactra, and AMT automobile "metalflake," "candy," and "pearlescent" paints in spray cans? In the late 1960s, Pactra introduced its International Color line of flat enamels for realistic aircraft camouflage colors.

Nowadays, you can get exactly the color you need from Floquil, Humbrol, Gunze Sangyo, Pactra, Polly S, Testor, Xtracolor, and others. These manufacturers all match their colors to the paints used on the full-size item. Most camouflage colors don't have to be mixed anymore; you just pull the exact paint you need right off the rack at the hobby shop.

Modeling paints come in many for-

mulas and colors, Table 1. They come in small bottles, usually about enough to paint two or three models. The old-time favorites are enamels, Fig. 2. Enamels are easy to stir, thin, and paint, and are the easiest to find. In the U. S., Pactra and Testor are the most familiar brands and can be found in dime stores as well as hobby shops. Many colors are available in spray cans which come in handy if you have one-color subjects and you need a finish devoid of brush marks.

Making inroads in this country are the British enamels made by Humbrol and Xtracolor. These paints are packaged in "tinlets," metal containers with pry-off lids. Unique among modeling paints, Xtracolor comes mixed to paint chip standards, but has a gloss surface. This eliminates the need for a clear gloss coat underneath decals (we'll have a lesson on decaling later). After decaling, a clear flat coat produces a realistic flat paint appearance.

Floquil is another long-standing brand, but unlike enamels, these paints are xylene-based, Fig. 3. Floquil should only be airbrushed onto plastic — hand brushing will produce a gummy mess because the solvent dissolves plastic. You could use Floquil's Barrier coat before hand brushing over plastic, but I find this to be more hassle than it's worth.

Enter acrylics. The most recent trend in model paints is "water-base" acrylics, Fig. 4. Although not necessarily nontoxic, acrylics are less hazardous than either enamels or lacquers. The original modeling acrylic is Polly S which comes in fantasy, railroad, and military camouflage colors.

Newcomers to the acrylic field are Tamiya and Gunze Sangyo Aqueous Hobby Color. Both of these Japanese paints are thinner than Polly S and require little dilution for airbrushing. Pactra Acrylics are also new and work well with little thinning.

In general, acrylics don't adhere to plastic as well as solvent-base paints. With this in mind, we have to make every effort to clean the model of oils and dust that would inhibit adhesion.

Thinners, and when to use them. Out of the bottle, most hobby paints are too thick to airbrush with good results. Without thinning, the paints spray with a grainy texture which hides detail. Thinners added to the paint lower the viscosity and make the paint flow through the airbrush and "atomize" easily into fine droplets.

There are many paint thinners and many can be used with more than one brand of paint. But for consistently good results, stick with the thinner made specifically for the brand of paint you use. If none is available, substitutions can be made. For example, Polly S Airbrush Thinner works fine with

Pactra and Gunze Sangyo paints, too. I've also had good luck using Floquil's Dio-sol with Testor, Humbrol, and Xtracolor enamels.

No matter what thinner you use, don't store thinned paint for more than a few days. Adding thinner upsets the balance of solvent, vehicle, and pigment and the mixture will eventually deteriorate and become unusable. For the same reason, never return thinned paint to the stock bottle. That'll ruin everything — usually just when you need that color!

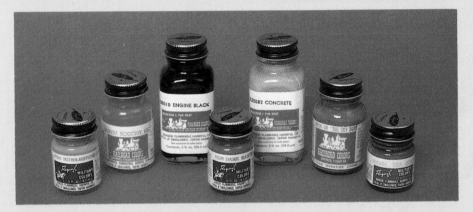

Fig. 3. Floquil started with a line of railroad paints, but now has military colors, many matched to Federal Standard 595a. Its xylene-base formula bites styrene slightly and should only be airbrushed with plenty of ventilation.

Fig. 4. Acrylics are the latest word in modeling paint. Most are water based and are safer to use than enamels or lacquers.

A word on safety. Paints and thinners should be treated as poisonous chemicals — even those labeled "nontoxic." I know what you're thinking — "no sweat, I'll never gulp down a bottle of paint." Yes, that's unlikely, but if you can detect the odor of paint, the harmful chemical is entering your body. Inhaling paint and thinner fumes can be as harmful as swallowing the stuff.

For most of us, painting outside is impractical, so make sure the area you paint in has really good ventilation — not just an open window. Invest in a spray booth, or at least an interchangeable-filter spray mask. You don't want your hobby to be the end of you.

Teacher's recommendations. For airbrushing, I prefer Floquil, but its strong solvent demands complete ventilation of the fumes. The same goes for enamels and acrylics thinned with alcohol. Without a doubt, my favorite paint for hand brushing is Polly S acrylic. Its thick consistency makes it easy to brush on. We'll discuss hand brushing in our next lesson. **FSM**

END LESSON 3

HOMEWORK ASSIGNMENT 3

Prepare your paint for painting

Materials: Your choice of modeling paints, compatible thinner, tube of beebees, and a rag.

☐ Reread this lesson.
☐ Check your paint supplies and discard dried-out or contaminated paints.
☐ Buy fresh paint.
☐ Prepare each bottle of paint by adding two beebees. Wipe off paint from bottle and cap threads and reseal.
☐ Don't thin paint yet.

Notice the striking Air Niugini markings on this 1/200 scale A-300 Airbus by Walt Fink of Crystal Lake, Illinois.

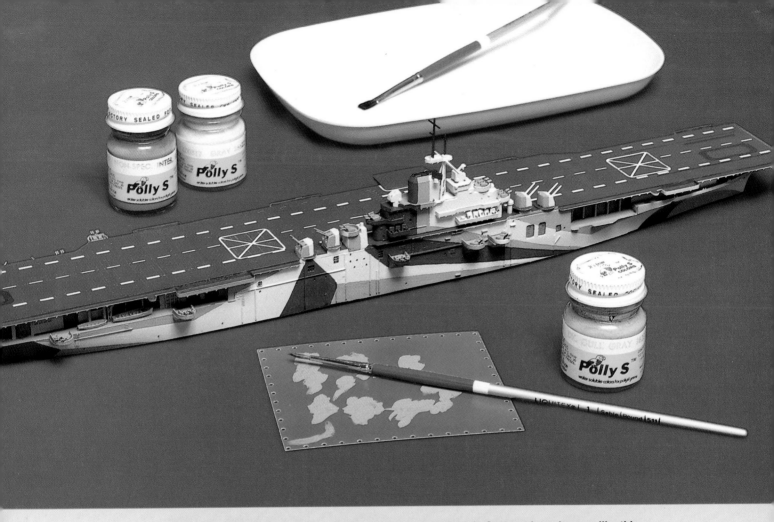

You don't need fancy painting equipment for a fancy paint job. Some paint schemes, like this "Dazzle" pattern on this 1/700 scale World War Two U. S. S. *Yorktown*, are easiest to apply with a brush.

LESSON 4:

Brush painting

It's not just for beginners

BY PAUL BOYER

IT'S TIME TO PAINT! Few models look good without paint — and the best-painted models look the best. Almost everyone starts painting models with a brush before trying spray cans or an airbrush. But brush painting shouldn't be considered amateurish — some of the best models and miniature figures I've seen were painted with brushes.

The big stumbling block with brush painting is eliminating brush marks — those annoying high and low spots created as the brush hairs distribute the paint on the model. The root cause of brush marks is that the paint has started to dry while the brushing action is still going on. The cure is good paint flow and knowing when to stop.

Choosing paintbrushes. Generally, the more you pay for a brush, the better quality you get. But don't spend a for-

tune; modeling paints, thinners, and rough duty will take their toll, and you'll be wasting money if you buy top-of-the-line brushes.

I use two types of brushes, Fig. 1: a No. 4 flat red sable (about ¼" wide) for broad areas, and a No. 1 round red sable that holds a good point for fine work. As these brushes get older, the hairs spread apart and begin to break off. When they do, I relegate them to more hazardous duty: applying liquid

16

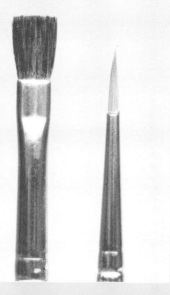

Fig. 1. Paul recommends a No. 4 flat red sable for covering broad areas, and a No. 1 round red sable that holds a good point.

Fig. 2. A drop or two of liquid dishwashing detergent acts as a wetting agent and allows water-based paint to flow better.

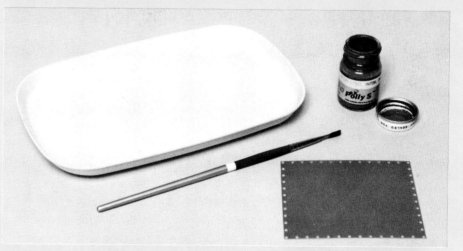

Fig. 3. Water in a plastic microwave/TV-dinner tray, a styrene palette, paints, and brushes are all you need to start hand brushing.

Fig. 4. Work the paint into the brush by stroking on the palette.

cement, dry-brushing, applying pastel chalks — even dusting off models!

Brush painting. In our last lesson we took a look at the different types of modeling paints. My favorite for hand brushing is Polly S acrylic. Why? First, Polly S is water based so no potentially harmful solvents are needed to clean up. Also, Polly S is thicker than other paints — it covers well and it's easy to apply.

As good as it is, Polly S paint isn't perfect. I add a couple drops of liquid dishwashing detergent to each new bottle, Fig. 2. The detergent is a wetting agent, reducing the surface tension of the paint, allowing it to flow better. (Don't add detergent to enamels or lacquers!) Drop in a pair of beebees, too, to serve as agitators when stirring and shaking.

The techniques we'll go through apply to Polly S paint — using enamels is similar, but substitute thinner for water. Ready? Let's go.

After thoroughly mixing the paint, open the bottle and place it behind or to the side of the model you're about to paint — you don't want to knock it over and spill paint all over the model. Now make a palette from a scrap of sheet styrene. Also set up a dish of water nearby, Fig. 3.

Dampen the brush in the water, then squeeze out excess water — you just want to moisten the hairs. Next, dip the brush into the bottle so that the hairs are halfway submerged in paint. With three or four short, quick strokes, spread the paint on the styrene palette, working the paint well into the brush hairs, Fig. 4.

Quickly transfer the loaded brush to the model and spread the paint on with

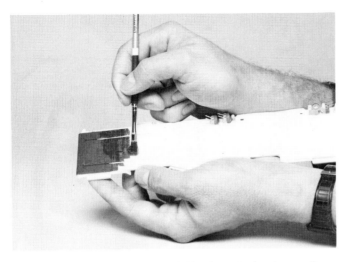

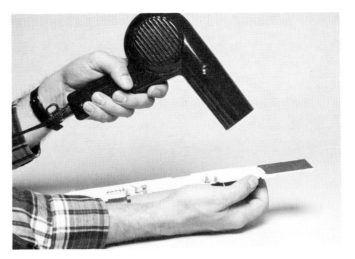

Fig. 5. Apply the paint to the model in short strokes in one direction to prevent brush marks.

Fig. 6. A hair dryer set on medium heat can accelerate the drying of Polly S paints.

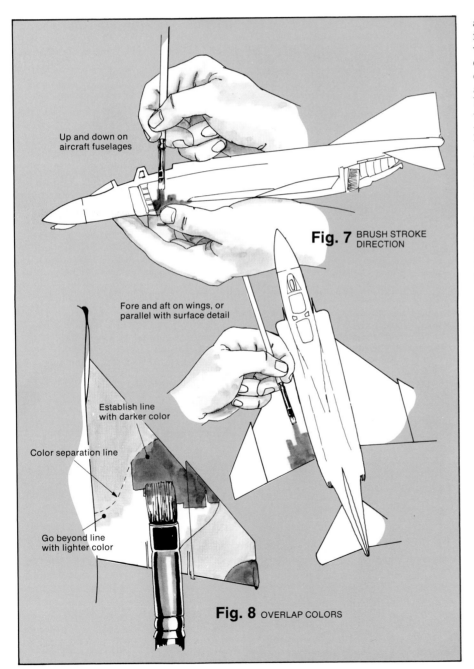

Up and down on aircraft fuselages

Fig. 7 BRUSH STROKE DIRECTION

Fore and aft on wings, or parallel with surface detail

Establish line with darker color

Color separation line

Go beyond line with lighter color

Fig. 8 OVERLAP COLORS

a few short strokes, no more than an inch long, Fig. 5. Although you don't want to glob on the paint, you also don't want to spread the paint too thin or too far — the paint will dry quickly and further brushing will only produce brush marks in the drying paint. As the brush begins to run out of paint, repeat the process. Cover a good-size area with a coat of paint; you may need another coat to cover completely but it's best to wait a few hours to prevent fresh paint from softening and lifting the underlying coat.

If the paint seems too thick or dries too quickly as you brush, dip the brush halfway in water before loading it with paint. Don't forget to work the paint into the brush hairs on your styrene palette every time.

To accelerate the drying of each coat, use a hair dryer set on medium heat, Fig. 6. Don't get too close and melt the model — 20 or 30 seconds of warm air will help cure Polly S.

Set up a brush stroke pattern. For aircraft fuselages, I stroke up and down, then fore and aft on the wings, in line with the airstream, Fig. 7. For other subjects, stroke parallel to surface detail. On our sample aircraft carrier, I stroked across the deck in line with the planks.

If the model you're painting will need many colors, always start with the lightest color and work your way to the darkest. Where different colors meet, paint the light color beyond the separation line, then establish the line with the dark color, Fig. 8. When you need to paint a specific area, outline it first with the No. 1 brush, then go back and fill the area with the flat brush, Fig. 9.

The second coat should be the final coat. When the second coat is dry, you should have uniform coverage and no brush marks.

Fine details. I use the No. 1 round

brush for fine details. It's important that the brush holds a sharp point. Tiny brushes (such as 000, 0000, or 00000) may have fine points, but they have few hairs and don't hold much paint. It's easier to load a No. 1, roll the brush on the palette to form the sharp point, then apply the paint to the model. If the paint in the tip dries, roll the hairs gently on the palette to bring fresh paint to the tip.

Cleanup. Certainly the beauty of Polly S paints is that you can clean the brushes with soap and water. However, don't let the paint dry on the brush for too long. Once Polly S has completely cured, it becomes impervious to water and you'll have to resort to strong solvents or brush cleaners which may damage the hairs.

Dip the dirty brush in water and roll the hairs against the inside of the dish, Fig. 10. Never pound the brush on the bottom of the dish as this damages the hairs. Next, apply a drop of liquid dishwashing detergent to the brush and massage the hairs for a minute. Flush it with fresh water and massage again. Gently squeeze excess water from the brush and form the point with your fingers. Store the brush with the hairs up, preferably with a protector, Fig. 11.

Don't let the brushes soak for more than a few minutes. Water (or thinner) can loosen the hairs inside the ferrule and swell the wood handle, loosening the ferrule, Fig. 12.

That pretty well covers it (ouch). Next lesson, we'll try spray cans. In the meantime, practice with your brushes.

FSM

END LESSON 4

HOMEWORK ASSIGNMENT 4
Painting with a brush

Materials: Polly S acrylic model paints, flat ¼"-wide red sable brush, No. 1 red sable brush with a good point, container of water, liquid dishwashing detergent, scrap plastic palette, hair dryer, assembled and primed model

☐ Reread this lesson.
☐ Add two drops of liquid detergent and two beebees to each bottle of paint.
☐ Stir and shake the paint thoroughly.
☐ Work paint into brush on plastic palette.
☐ Spread paint on model with short, quick strokes — lightest color first.
☐ Accelerate drying with hair dryer.
☐ Apply second coat if necessary.
☐ Clean brushes thoroughly.
☐ Store brushes properly.

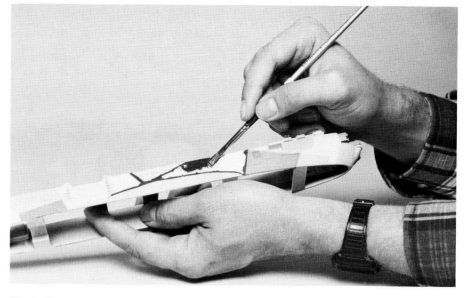
Fig. 9. The fine brush is used to outline the color area, then the wide brush fills it in.

Fig. 10. To clean the brush, gently roll it in the water up against the side of the dish.

Fig. 11. Always place the clear protector over the brush to keep the hairs from being damaged.

Fig. 12. This brush has had it! The hairs splay out, paint is clogged at the ferrule, and the handle is swollen and cracked. You can use it to apply pastels or for dry-brushing, but not for painting.

Spray cans are ideal for painting model cars like this 1/24 scale Monogram 1956 Thunderbird.

LESSON 5:

Painting with spray cans

Achieve beautiful finishes quickly and easily

BY PAUL BOYER

THE NEXT LOGICAL step in our study of model finishing techniques is to learn all about the ever-popular spray can. Those of you who have experience in graffiti are familiar with this little item. I won't need assistance demonstrating this technique, thank you.

If you don't like brush painting and are inexperienced with an airbrush, spray cans may be just what you're looking for. Spray cans are ideal for single-color subjects, or multicolored models that can be easily masked.

The anatomy of the aerosol can. A spray can is simply thinned paint along with a compressed-gas propellant inside a sealed metal container. Now you ask, "What's that rattle?" Also packed inside is a small ball bearing that works as an agitator (just like the beebees we put in paint bottles). Shaking the can rattles the ball bearing around, mixing the heavy pigment with the lighter ve-

hicle and solvent. Pressing the valve at the top of the can allows the paint and propellant to exit. The compressed gas pushes the paint up the siphon tube and out the valve, Fig. 1.

Since the siphon tube may be curved and because the paint settles to the lowest part of the can, you may have to turn the can to get every drop of paint out of it. Rotate the valve so you can spray in the right direction, too. When you're finished painting, turn the can upside down and press the valve for a

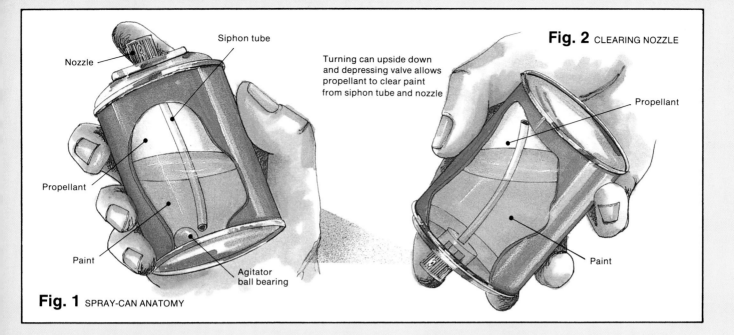

Nozzle

Siphon tube

Turning can upside down
and depressing valve allows
propellant to clear paint
from siphon tube and nozzle

Fig. 2 CLEARING NOZZLE

Propellant

Propellant

Paint

Paint

Agitator
ball bearing

Fig. 1 SPRAY-CAN ANATOMY

Fig. 3. To catch overspray, place the model inside a large cardboard box.

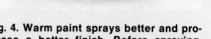

Fig. 4. Warm paint sprays better and produces a better finish. Before spraying, warm the can in a jar of hot tap water.

few seconds. The paint will fall to the top of the can and clear propellant will travel down the siphon and out the valve — a self-cleaning valve, Fig. 2.

Avoiding toxic fumes. As innocent and harmless as spray paint may seem, the chemicals involved in most paint formulas are toxic. Xylene, toluol, benzene, and a plateful of mouthfuls like these are found in model paints. None of them is good for you so you'll want to avoid getting the paint on your skin and the fumes in your lungs. If you can, spray outdoors. You won't have to file an environmental impact statement for the small amount of overspray involved in painting models, but watch

out for overspray drifting toward your car, garden, house, or pets.

If you must spray indoors, rig a large cardboard box to catch overspray, Fig. 3. This won't take the fumes out of the air, though, so ventilate the area; you don't want your hobby to be the end of you.

Painting with a spray can. My favorite application for spray cans is painting model cars. With care, I can get terrific gloss finishes more easily and quickly than with an airbrush. With care — that's the trick.

First warm the spray can. Leave it for a few minutes in water drawn from your hot water faucet, Fig. 4. You should be able to dip your finger in the water without scalding yourself. DON'T

put the can in water in a pot on the stove! Also, DON'T try to heat the can in the microwave! Warm paint sprays better and settles on the surface more smoothly. If you remember your high school physics, a compressed gas cools as it is released, so warming the paint helps counteract this effect.

For years, modelers have used the ubiquitous wire coat hanger to hold models while spraying — I can't think of anything better for holding car bodies. You can bend and shape the hanger any which way. I try to form a rectangle that will fit inside the body and a handle that doubles as a stand, Fig. 5. The idea is to hold the model from the inside while you spray and while the

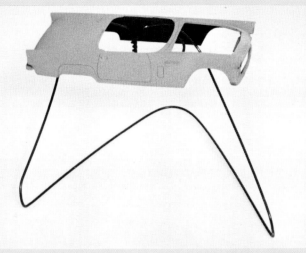

Fig. 5. A wire coat hanger can be bent to form a holder for hands-off spraying.

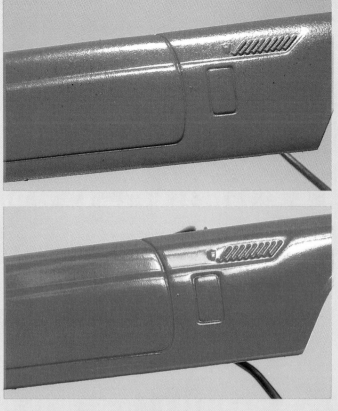

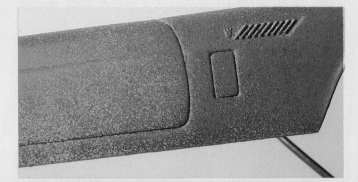

Fig. 7. (Left) The first coat should be just a dusting to provide "tooth" for the second coat (top) which produces an "orange peel" finish. (Above) The third and final coat for gloss paint should be a wet, heavy application, but not so heavy that it causes runs.

paint dries. To hold small parts, attach a loop of masking tape with the sticky side out to cardboard, then press the parts to the tape.

Now let's paint. Spray cans pump out quite a volume of paint in a short time, making it all too easy to apply too much paint too fast, which leads to runs and obscured detail. Resist the temptation to cover the model with a solid, wet coat — this isn't lawn furniture we're painting!

When spraying, hold the can between 6″ and 12″ from the model. Always keep the can moving. Start spraying off the model, move the spray over the model, then release the valve off the model, Fig. 6. As the valve is released, a little paint builds up at the orifice and is blown off in large droplets the next time you depress the valve. You want the model to receive only fine paint droplets — those big droplets will cause uneven spots in the finish.

The first coat should be a dusting that doesn't quite cover the surface, Fig. 7. The fine spray droplets will be able to grab the plastic or primer and provide "tooth" for subsequent coats.

Dust: the enemy. Inspect the model for dust particles. Dust is a fact of life that will always affect painting models. To avoid dust, make sure the model and the area you're spraying in are as clean as possible. When (note that I didn't say "if") you get dust on the freshly painted model, carefully pick it out with sharp-pointed tweezers or by carefully touching masking tape to the area while the paint is still wet. Subsequent coats should cover any marks made by the tweezers or tape. Don't use a rag or a cotton swab to remove dust particles from fresh paint! The fibers will stick to the paint and make a bigger mess.

Let the first dusting coat dry for about 20 minutes, then apply the second coat. This time you want to cover the model with a slightly heavier coat. For flat paints, this second coat should be all you need. On gloss surfaces, you should see a shiny, but not yet smooth surface. This sheen is called "orange peel," named for the shiny but dimpled surface of an orange. Set the model aside for another 20 minutes.

Now comes the critical third and final coat of a glossy finish. Apply a wet,

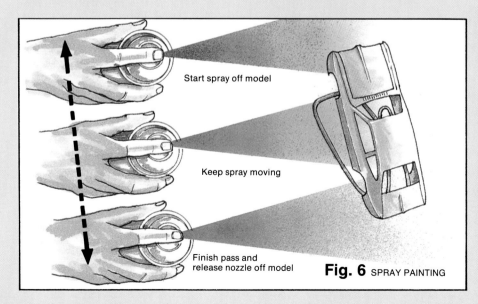

Start spray off model

Keep spray moving

Finish pass and release nozzle off model

Fig. 6 SPRAY PAINTING

Fig. 8. After the final coat, park the model underneath a box to prevent dust particles from settling in the fresh paint.

almost heavy, coat this time. Be sure to keep the can moving and don't start or finish your strokes on the model. You don't want to load the paint on so heavy that it runs. Check the model for runs after every pass.

If you cause a run, stop! Applying more paint to even things out will only make more runs. Position the model so that the area with the run is horizontal, allowing the excess paint to spread over the largest area possible. Put the model under cover and don't touch it for at least three days — that's how long it will take for the paint to dry.

If you discover a run *after* the paint is dry, try sanding it down with 600-grit wet-or-dry sandpaper followed by either rubbing compound, plastic polish, or toothpaste. That's right, toothpaste contains a fine abrasive. It also gives you the freshest model on the table!

After you've finished applying the third coat, place the model on your workbench and cover it with a box, Fig. 8. To keep dust from falling on the fresh paint, use a sprayer bottle to dampen the inside of the box with water. The box shouldn't make an airtight drying compartment, but it will prevent dust and lint from settling on the fresh paint.

If you've used flat paint, allow the model to dry for 24 hours before handling. If it's gloss paint, leave it in the box for 2 or 3 days. Gloss paints take a while to dry, and nothing ruins a model's appearance more than a glossy paint job with fingerprints.

Good timing. There is an important time factor for successful spray painting. You should apply subsequent coats within 3 hours of each other. If you can't fit your next coat into that time period, wait at least 36 hours before ap-

plying the next coat. What happens in between? The paint cures. If you add another coat during that time, you run the risk of lifting the earlier coats — and that's bad. It'll look like chips and flakes underneath the top coat. If you do have to wait 36 hours, lightly sand the earlier coat to provide a better grip for the new coat.

END LESSON 5

HOMEWORK ASSIGNMENT 5

Painting with a spray can

Materials: Model ready to paint (Lesson 3), can of spray paint, wire coat hangers, large cardboard box, masking tape, fine-pointed tweezers

- [ ] Reread this lesson.
- [ ] If spraying inside, rig cardboard box to catch overspray.
- [ ] Mount model on wire coat hanger bent to hold model from the inside.
- [ ] Warm spray can in hot tap water.
- [ ] Shake the can vigorously for one minute so ball bearing inside mixes contents.
- [ ] Apply first light coat; don't try to cover the model with the first coat. Hold can 6″ to 12″ from model. Always start and stop spray off the model.
- [ ] Inspect for and remove dust particles with tweezers or tape.
- [ ] After waiting at least 20 minutes but no more than 3 hours, apply second coat. If using gloss paint, you should get an "orange peel" finish.
- [ ] Check again for dust.
- [ ] Wait another 20 minutes, then apply third and final coat (for gloss paints).
- [ ] Check for runs after every pass.
- [ ] Check again for dust.
- [ ] Rest model on workbench and cover with a box.
- [ ] Clean spray can nozzle by holding the can upside down and depressing valve.
- [ ] Don't touch the model for 1 day (flat paint), or 3 days (gloss paint).

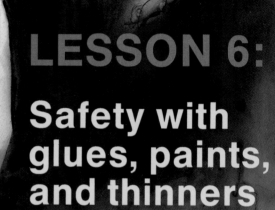

LESSON 6:

Safety with glues, paints, and thinners

Do you know the hazards?

Do you know the dangers you face using common modeling materials? If mishandled, some can be dangerous — even deadly! Guest lecturer Ross Martinek suggests some simple precautions.

GUEST LECTURER: ROSS MARTINEK

WELL, BY NOW you are modeling veterans, right? After five lessons, you're nearly halfway through the course. You're enjoying your hobby more and you're feeling confident. But I'm going to shake that confidence a little, perhaps make you worry, and that's good. Hey, what are guest lecturers for, anyway?

Who, since you started this course, has read the warning labels on each brand of glue, paint, and thinner you use? I thought so. All right, can anyone tell me about the potential dangers you face when you use them? Dizziness, hmmm. Nausea — well, these are only symptoms, nature's little ways of telling you that something is wrong. The danger we all face using these materials is chemical toxicity — poison.

Now, I don't want to scare you off from building models. As hobbies go, this is one of the safest. But too many modelers ignore the potential hazards of the materials they use to make every model. Most of these substances demand more respect than they receive.

This lecture will not only tell you *why* to be careful with these materials, but *how* to be careful. A few simple, inexpensive precautions can help protect you.

Terms. Sometimes it's hard to say which chemicals are dangerous. New compounds are being produced at a fantastic rate, and toxicology research cannot keep up. Material not proven to be toxic may not be required to carry warning labels, or may only be required to carry limited cautionary statements. Furthermore, any material not required to be labeled as toxic can be labeled as

Fig. 1. Chemical cartridge respirators like these have two-stage filtration specifically designed to protect against organic vapors. At left is model No. 8725 from the Occupational Health and Safety Products Division of 3M, 220-7W 3M Center, St. Paul, MN 55144. It costs about $15.00 and is disposable. The Glenaire Respirator (right) is sold by Badger Airbrush Co., 9128 W. Belmont Ave., Franklin Park, IL 60131 (as No. 190-1). It costs around $30.00 and has replaceable cartridges and prefilters.

Table 1: Chemistry of common modeling materials

Modeling material	Chemicals
Tube cements	Toluene, acetone, allyl isothiocyanate (oil of mustard), trichloroethane, methyl isobutyl ketone, methyl cellosolve acetate, methyl ethyl ketone
Liquid solvent cements	Methyl cellosolve acetate, methyl isobutyl ketone, methyl ethyl ketone, tetrahydrofuran, triethanolamine, trichloroethane, methylene chloride
Filler putties	Toluene, xylene, acetone, alcohols, methyl isobutyl ketone, methyl cellosolve acetate, trichloroethane, methylene chloride, methyl ethyl ketone
Paint thinners and solvents	Acetone, toluene, xylene, alcohols, mineral spirits, methyl ethyl ketone, turpentine, methylene chloride
Paints	Toluene, xylene, acetone, mineral spirits, turpentine, triethanolamine, organic amines, alcohols, methylene chloride, propylene glycol, butyl acetate, tributylphosphate, octyl alcohol
Super glues	Cyanoacrylate esters
Accelerators for super glues	Triethanolamine, other organic amines

nontoxic! Obviously, manufacturers are not always the definitive source for hazard information.

What makes a substance toxic? Obviously, its composition is the prime factor, but the degree and the duration of the exposure to the material work into the equation, too. Take a look at Tables 1 and 2. Table 1 tells you what chemicals are included in most of the modeling materials you use. Table 2 tells you the dangers of those chemicals. Now, you won't need to memorize the tables, but you should keep them as references to help you understand the potential hazards.

Note that not all of the chemicals listed for a given material may be present in all types or brands. Also, some of these chemicals are present only in small amounts. Please consider these tables as illustrative — they are by no means complete or definitive.

What may be hazardous today could be determined harmless (or deadly) tomorrow.

Throughout the tables you'll see words that need explaining in layman's terms. First, "carcinogen" — no doubt you've heard this one on the news. It's a substance that causes cancer. There are no dosage levels for carcinogens — a single molecule *may* cause cancer, especially if it is a strong carcinogen. On the other hand, massive exposure may not harm you. Why? It depends on the carcinogen involved, your vulnerability, and a host of other factors. Any carcinogen *may* cause cancer, but it's difficult to say who, how, and when. We all know that sunlight is necessary for good health, yet it is a known carcinogen — too much and you could get skin cancer. Sensible people avoid strong carcinogens, and limit their exposure to the weaker ones.

"Suspected carcinogen" is a material thought to cause cancer, but I couldn't find documented evidence for the claims. "Possible carcinogen" describes a material that is believed to be carcinogenic, and has documented evidence to support the claim.

Materials labeled as "highly toxic" should be used with great care, as they may easily cause death or permanent injury at relatively low dosage levels.

Those labeled as "moderately toxic" usually don't cause permanent injury or death, although they may cause irreversible changes to exposed tissues, and could cause severe discomfort.

"Low toxicity" materials generally cause readily reversible tissue changes and some discomfort.

"Narcotic" describes the *effect* of a material on the body — these materials are not narcotics or drugs in the usual sense. Their effects can include symptoms resembling deep sleep and possible depression of vital functions.

An "allergen" is a substance which triggers an allergic response. A "teratogen" causes birth defects. The teratogenic properties of many chemicals are not well known. Pregnant women should consult a physician about exposure to any chemical. A "sensitizer" makes you more sensitive to itself and to other chemicals.

All of the information is for "acute" exposure unless other exposure conditions are given. Acute exposure means of short duration — seconds, minutes, or hours for skin absorption or inhalation, or a single ingested dose. I could find no studies on the combined effects of multiple exposures to many different toxins and carcinogens.

Other materials. I didn't list polyester (casting) resins as there are so many of them, and their toxicity varies. Since the uncured resins may contain toxic additives, and many of the hardeners are potentially dangerous, you should treat them as toxic substances. Always wear gloves and a proper respirator, and provide adequate ventilation when using polyester resins.

Polycarbonates (acrylics including Lucite and Plexiglas) are reported to be nontoxic. Except for methylene chloride, I was unable to find information on the toxicity of polycarbonate adhesives — treat them with caution.

I want to clear the air about cyanoacrylate glues — super glues. They are not typical of compounds containing the root word "cyan," which means a cyanide compound. Although these glues and their fumes can be irritating to the eyes, nose, and throat, they do not contain cyanide, nor do they decompose into poisonous cyanide compounds when they set or are heated. Cyanoacrylates were first developed for surgical appli-

Fig. 2. Nitrile rubber gloves can help protect you from hazardous chemicals. These can be found in hardware stores and cost less than $5.00.

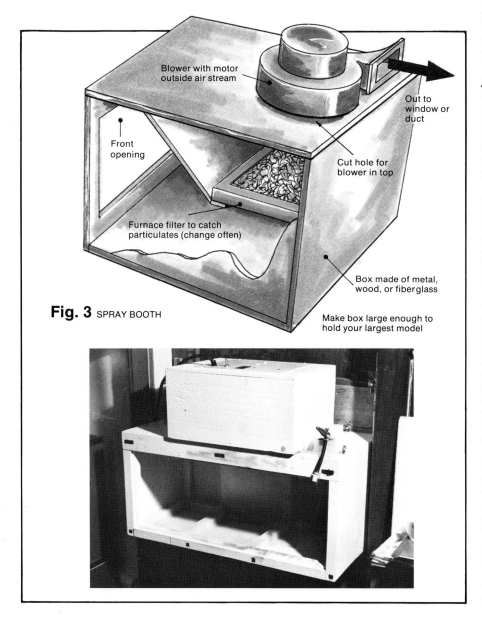

Blower with motor outside air stream

Out to window or duct

Front opening

Cut hole for blower in top

Furnace filter to catch particulates (change often)

Box made of metal, wood, or fiberglass

Fig. 3 SPRAY BOOTH

Make box large enough to hold your largest model

cations — which explains why they are so good at bonding skin!

Safety and prevention. You should consider the information in the tables carefully. I try to be conservative — I take more precautions than the published toxicity information calls for. Do not assume that a material is harmless just because it is labeled nontoxic, or carries no warning labels. Exercise reasonable care when handling materials you know little or nothing about, and great care with materials you know are hazardous.

Adequate ventilation, a respirator, rubber gloves, and hygiene are good, inexpensive countermeasures.

How much ventilation is adequate? Adequate ventilation is not two open windows, an open window and an open door, or a fan in the corner. A good rule of thumb is if you or someone else in the building can smell the materials you're working with, the ventilation is NOT adequate. But, this rule doesn't work if the material is odorless. A respirator with organic vapor cartridges, Fig. 1, is a partial fix for inadequate ventilation, since it protects only the wearer.

Since absorption through the skin is just as dangerous as inhalation, you should protect your hands from solvent chemicals. Wear nitrile rubber gloves, found in hardware stores, when you use these solvents, Fig. 2. Disposable surgical gloves don't offer enough protection — some of the chemicals can pass through latex and to your skin.

If you get paint on your skin, don't remove it with paint thinner — it takes the paint off, but the thinner may be even more hazardous. Wipe away as much of the paint as you can with a rag, then use a commercially available hand cleaner or an abrasive soap and a lot of elbow grease.

Wash your hands before and after working on a model. Don't eat or drink while handling toxic material. Don't smoke or use open flames around paints, thinners, and other solvent chemicals. Many of these materials are flammable and that cigarette could cause a flash fire or explosion. When burned, many otherwise harmless materials produce toxic fumes. Make sure that everything is capped tight before lighting your sprue-stretching candle.

Your best protection — a spray booth. Nothing will protect you and those around you from toxic fumes as well as a spray booth. I don't mean a cardboard box, but you probably don't need an industrial behemoth, either. You can build your own spray booth, but make sure it is big enough to hold the largest model part you plan to paint.

The diagram and photos in Fig. 3 show the spray booth I made from scrounged materials, but you can make one out of almost anything — wood, sheet metal, even fiberglass if you have the experience. With little adaptation, this unit will fit into just about any window.

To increase the fire resistance of my wood spray booth, I coated it with fiberglass resin. Realistically, the booth's fire resistance isn't a major concern — you're not going to use it as an exhaust for an oven. If the booth catches fire, you were in deep trouble long before that.

The key to an efficient spray booth is to place the unit as close to the outside air as possible — preferably in a window. Ducting the air requires a more powerful fan. Any turns in the ductwork slow the passage of air.

Picking a fan. The most important component of any spray booth is the exhaust fan. The purpose of a spray booth is to evacuate fumes as efficiently as possible. According to Andy Sperandeo's "Safety in painting" article (November 1987 *Model Railroader*), the Environmental Protection Agency and the Occupational Safety and Health Administration (OSHA) recommend that a spray booth have an air flow rate of 100 to 200 linear feet per minute.

Since fans and blowers are rated by the *cubic* feet of air they move in one minute (cfm), you first have to determine the size of the front opening of the spray booth. Let's say we want our spray booth to have an air flow of 200 linear feet per minute, and that the front of the booth is 2' wide by 1' high. Determine the area of the opening by multiplying the width by the height. Multiply this by the desired flow (200) and you can determine the rating of the fan you'll need for your booth:

2' x 1' x 200 fm = 400 cfm.

This equation is good for a booth without ducting. If you must run ducting from the exhaust fan, the area of cross section of the duct should be no smaller than the area of the cross section of the fan outlet for efficient performance.

When you purchase a fan, make sure the motor is outside the air stream to decrease the chance of sparks igniting flammable fumes. Although they are not rated "explosion proof," we recommend Dayton model No. 4C445A (rated at 525 cfm) and No. 2C946 (rated at 815 cfm). Use the more powerful fan if your duct is smaller than 5" in diameter, if your duct is longer than 6', or if you have more than two 90-degree bends in the duct. Dayton blowers are available from W. W. Grainger Inc. stores across the country, or call Dayton at (708) 647-0124 to find a dealer near you. If you can't find these blowers, buy something equally as powerful to be sure the harmful fumes are removed from your workshop.

Again, be thoughtful and concerned,

Table 2: Chemical toxicology (See text for definitions.)

Chemical	Toxicology
Acetone	Narcotic in high concentrations. Defatting (degreasing) action can cause skin irritation. Hazard to eyes from defatting action.
Allyl isothiocyanate	Highly toxic (see comments in text on "-cyan-"). Allergen. May cause contact dermatitis.
Butyl acetate	Moderate irritant to respiratory system and mucous membranes. Mild allergen.
Cyanoacrylate esters	Skin, eye, and respiratory irritant.
Epoxy resins, incompletely cured	Most cured resins have little or no toxic effects. However, their curing compounds (hardeners) frequently contain organic amines which are HIGHLY toxic and sometimes carcinogenic. Uncured resin is a possible carcinogen.
Ethyl alcohol (ethanol)	"Good 'ol Hooch" (drinking alcohol) unless denatured, in which case see methyl alcohol. You can also inhale it in sufficient amounts to become intoxicated without your knowledge or consent.
Isopropyl alcohol	Stronger narcotic than methyl alcohol. Can cause eye damage by contact. Single lethal dose is 250 ml; however, as little as 10 ml taken internally have caused serious illness. Absorbed by skin.
Lacquer thinners	See toluene, xylene, methyl ethyl ketone, and trichloroethane.
Methyl alcohol (methanol)	Not considered highly toxic, but the damage it causes is severe. A cumulative poison (like arsenic and lead). Can be absorbed by inhalation and by skin contact, but is more toxic if inhaled. Possible carcinogen.
Methyl cellosolve acetate (MCA)	Highly toxic if ingested. Moderately toxic for other chronic exposures.
Methyl ethyl ketone (MEK)	Moderately toxic by oral routes; low toxicity by dermal (skin) routes. Teratogen. Strong irritant.
Methyl isobutyl ketone	Highly toxic (narcotic) if ingested or inhaled. Eye and respiratory irritant.
Methylene chloride	Extremely narcotic. Skin penetrant. Causes severe damage to eyes on contact. Carcinogen.
Mineral spirits	Moderately toxic. Also an irritant.
Octyl alcohol	Moderately toxic when absorbed through skin or ingested.
Organic amines	Some are highly toxic, many are skin irritants, some are sensitizers. Some are carcinogens.
PVC cement	See tetrahydrofuran.
PVC cleaner	See trichloroethane and tetrahydrofuran.
Trichloroethane (1-1-1)	Narcotic in high concentrations. Moderately toxic. May cause liver and kidney damage. A suspected carcinogen.
Styrene	Vapors (from heating) irritating to eyes and respiratory system, and mildly narcotic. Fumes from melting and burning are possible carcinogen.
Tetrahydrofuran (THF)	Extremely toxic. Causes kidney and liver damage. Irritating to eyes and respiratory system.
Toluene (toluol)	Moderately toxic. A suspected carcinogen.
Tributylphosphate	Highly to moderately toxic. Affects central nervous system.
Triethanolamine (TEA)	A suspected carcinogen. Allergen. Reported low oral toxicity.
Turpentine	Highly toxic. Can cause serious irritation of the kidneys if ingested. Strong irritant. Allergen. Possible carcinogen.
Vinyl acetate	Fumes from burning or heating are toxic.
Vinyl butyrate	Fumes from burning or heating are toxic.
Vinyl chloride (PVC)	Vinyl chloride liquid is highly toxic if inhaled or absorbed by skin. Carcinogen. Polymer (PVC) is less dangerous unless heated to decomposition. PVC is an allergen.
Xylene (xylol)	Moderately toxic. A suspected carcinogen.

but don't be scared off. Modeling is one of the safest hobbies. Be careful and keep it that way. Thanks for your time, and now your instructor will give you your homework assignment.

Thank you Ross. As usual, I want you to read over this lesson and study the tables. Consider the risks involved and take this advice seriously.

FSM's Finishing School will take a two-issue summer vacation and will return in the November issue with our first of two lessons on airbrushing. See you then. Class dismissed. *Paul Boyer*
FSM

ADDITIONAL READING

• Sax, N. Irving, *Dangerous Properties of Industrial Materials*, Van Nostrand Reinhold, New York, 1975 (4th edition or later)
• Sperandeo, Andrew, "Safety in Painting," *Model Railroader*, November 1987, Kalmbach Publishing Co., Waukesha, Wisconsin
• Sperandeo, Andrew, "The Paint Shop Spray Booth," *Model Railroader*, January 1988, Kalmbach Publishing Co., Waukesha, Wisconsin
• Wesolowski, Wayne and Mary Kay, *ABCs of Building Model Railroad Cars* (chapter 4, "Safety and the Hobbyist,") Tab Books Inc., Blue Ridge Summit, Pennsylvania, 1985

Note the victory notches on this finely weathered 1/32 scale Hellcat by Greg Granrath of West Allis, Wisconsin.

For many modelers, an airbrush is the paint applicator of choice. Once you get the hang of it, airbrushing is easy.

LESSON 7:

Basic airbrushing

Getting started with the ideal paint applicator

BY PAUL BOYER

WELCOME BACK, everyone. I hope you enjoyed your summer off. No, I won't ask you to write a theme on what you did for summer vacation. Sorry to disappoint you. If you're like me, you probably didn't get much modeling in while the weather was good, but that didn't keep you from visiting your local hobby shop and stocking up for the winter.

I wonder how many of you purchased an airbrush recently. Hands, please. Aha, quite a few of you. Have you had a chance to use it? How many of you were successful in your first attempt? I didn't think so. Well, don't give up. Like everything else in this hobby, you will get better at airbrushing with practice. And practice and more practice.

What is an airbrush? An airbrush is simply a miniature spray gun, a device that mixes air and paint to spray an even coat of color. Paint in a reservoir is drawn through a needle valve by the vacuum created when air blows across the orifice of the nozzle, Fig. 1. The rushing air blows paint off the tip of the needle in a fine mist.

There are two types of airbrushes. A single-action airbrush has separate controls to regulate air flow and adjust paint volume. A double-action (or dual-action) airbrush has one button that controls both air and paint volume. Depressing the button releases the air; rocking the button back increases paint volume, Fig. 2.

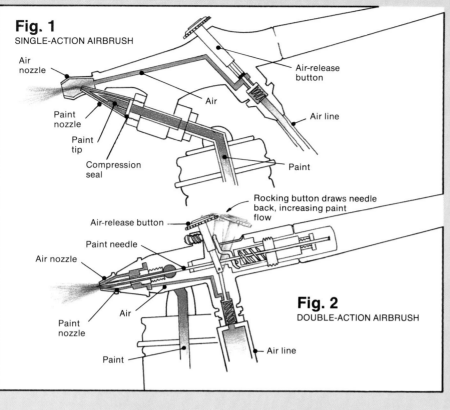

Fig. 1
SINGLE-ACTION AIRBRUSH

Air nozzle

Paint nozzle

Paint tip

Compression seal

Air

Air-release button

Air line

Paint

Rocking button draws needle back, increasing paint flow

Air-release button

Paint needle

Air nozzle

Air

Paint nozzle

Paint

Air line

Fig. 2
DOUBLE-ACTION AIRBRUSH

Fig. 3. Most modelers use a simple compressor to supply air to the airbrush.

Fig. 4. A cylinder of compressed CO_2 is expensive but quiet and easy to regulate.

Fig. 5. Cans of propellant are available in many hobby shops. In the long run, they are expensive.

Fig. 6. To keep the airbrush from blowing small parts from your work table, stick the parts on masking tape rolled over on itself.

Most single-action airbrushes mix air and paint outside the nozzle and are sometimes called external-mix airbrushes. Most double-action airbrushes mix air and paint inside the nozzle and are called internal-mix airbrushes, but the distinction between internal and external is fuzzy and we'll stick with the single-action and double-action labels.

Although double-action airbrushes can produce finer lines than single-action airbrushes, they are expensive, difficult to master, and harder to clean. For painting models, single-action airbrushes work fine, and today's lesson will concentrate on using this type.

Of course you'll need compressed gas to spray with an airbrush. Sources for this vary, but most modelers use a compressor run by an electric motor, Fig. 3. A piston or diaphragm inside the compressor squeezes air into a small-diam-

eter hose to the airbrush where it is forced through a tiny orifice in the nozzle. Other sources include compressed air or carbon dioxide (CO_2) in cylinders, Fig. 4, and small propellant cans, Fig. 5. Each of these air sources has its advantages and disadvantages: Compressors are relatively inexpensive and easy to use, but they are noisy and you usually can't regulate the air pressure. Propellant cans don't require a major initial investment and can be used anywhere, but they don't hold much gas and, in the long run, they're expensive. I prefer a cylinder of CO_2; it's quiet and easy to regulate, even though the initial cost is high and the cylinder must be refilled periodically.

Airbrushing 101. Airbrushing is often seen as the technique that separates serious modelers from beginners. This really isn't so, but you may find that with experience it's easier to produce better paint jobs with an airbrush than with any other technique. Note I said "with experience." I know of no modeler who mastered (or even enjoyed) painting with an airbrush on his first attempt.

Let's first prepare the work area for airbrushing. As you learned in our les-

son at the end of last semester (May 1990 FSM), for safety's sake you must evacuate all paint and thinner fumes from your work area. Although there is little overspray from a properly used airbrush, you should still scan your work area for finished models, open books, decal sheets, family treasures, and anything else that could be damaged by overspray. Tuck them away or remove them from the room altogether. Anchor tiny parts to your work surface with tape rolled over on itself, Fig. 6.

Most hobby paints (whether enamels, acrylics, or lacquers) need to be thinned to spray effectively through the airbrush. While you're learning, use the thinner recommended by the paint manufacturer. There's no set amount of thinner to use — each paint will differ, but I start with two parts paint to one part thinner. For airbrushing, paint should be thinned to the consistency of dairy half-and-half. Mix the paint and thinner in a separate container (I use plastic 35 mm film canisters), then pour the mixture into the airbrush paint bottle or color cup. If you're using the color cup, don't fill it all the way as it spills easily. To help prevent clogging, pour the paint mix-

Fig. 7. A siphon strainer keeps lumps of paint from clogging the airbrush.

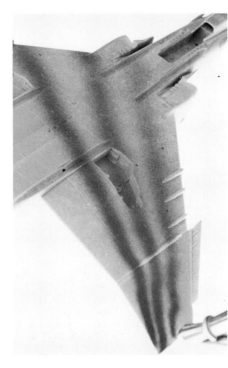

Fig. 9. The closer you come to the surface, the tighter and stronger the spray pattern.

Fig. 10. When sprayed at a 45-degree angle, the spray pattern becomes tight at the bottom and wide at the top. This will come in handy when spraying camouflage patterns freehand.

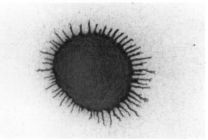

Fig. 11. Oops! Too close or too much paint. You'll need to back off or close the paint control valve.

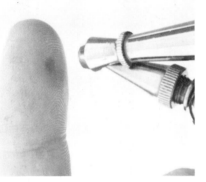

Fig. 8. To get the "feel" of the airbrush's spray pattern, close the paint valve and blow air on your finger.

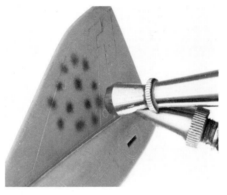

Fig. 12. With practice and properly thinned paint, you'll be able to create tiny dots such as these with a single-action airbrush.

ture through fine cheesecloth or invest in a siphon strainer that fits into the airbrush paint bottle, Fig. 7.

Most thinned model paints can be airbrushed with air pressure between 15 and 30 psi (pounds per square inch). Most hobby compressors don't allow you to regulate air pressure, but provide enough pressure to operate the airbrush.

Ready, aim, spray! Now all we need is a target. The best way to practice airbrushing is to experiment on an old model. I don't recommend spraying on paper or cardboard for practice; you may find that the spray pattern and paint-to-thinner ratio you're using may work fine on paper, but when you spray the model, the paint runs. That's because paint is absorbed by paper and cardboard, but not by plastic or metal.

Start by turning on the compressor, closing the paint valve, and depressing the air-release button. Hold your hand about 3″ in front of the airbrush and get an idea of the air flow pattern coming out of the nozzle. Move your hand in toward the airbrush. As you draw closer, you'll feel the spray pattern become smaller and stronger. When your hand is about ½″ away, the air stream feels like an invisible pencil point on your skin, Fig. 8. Remember this.

Now open the paint valve about two full turns. Get your hand out of the way this time and spray the model. Again start about 3″ away and as you paint perpendicular to the model's surface, bring the airbrush closer. See how the spray pattern becomes smaller as you move closer to the surface. Also, notice how the color becomes

stronger, Fig. 9. Remember this, too.

Now make another pass, but this time tilt the surface of the model 45 degrees to the airbrush. Again start 3″ away and move in. Notice how the spray pattern is elliptical and how the bottom edge is stronger and more distinct than the top edge, Fig. 10. This characteristic is important and will come in handy when you paint camouflage patterns in our next lesson.

I see spots. Gaining control of the airbrush takes time, but there are exercises that can help you. Open the paint control one full turn from fully closed. Position the airbrush so that the nozzle is about ½″ away from the surface, depress the air button, and spray a dot of color. If the paint creates a little splash, Fig. 11, close the paint control valve a little more. Repeat this procedure until you can create a tiny dot, Fig. 12.

Keeping the airbrush the same distance from the model, try writing your name. Most likely about halfway through writing, the paint will stop flowing. What happened? The small opening restricts the paint flow and the tip eventually clogs, stopping the flow. It's difficult to avoid clogging, but you can fix it. Wet a cotton swab with thinner and wipe the tip, then spray away from the model to clear the clog. Not as effective is to open the color control valve another turn, spray away from

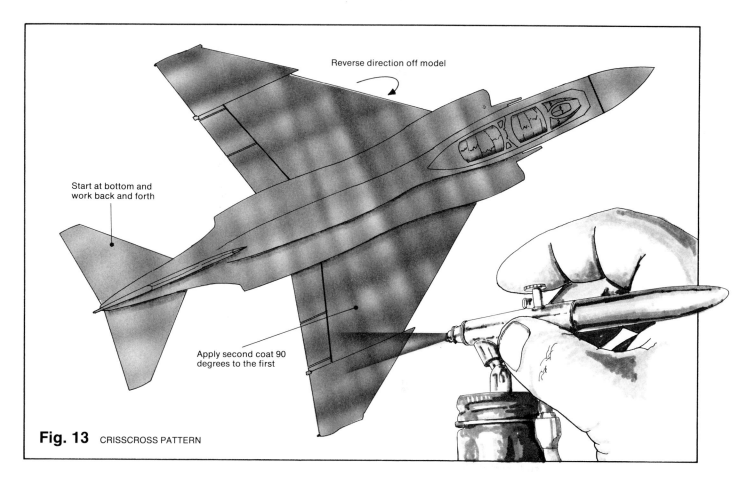

Reverse direction off model

Start at bottom and work back and forth

Apply second coat 90 degrees to the first

Fig. 13 CRISSCROSS PATTERN

the model, then close the valve to your original setting and continue.

Coverage. Don't expect the airbrush to cover a model with paint as quickly as a spray can will. The paint droplets should reach the model just before they start to dry. The sprayed area should look wet for a few seconds, then the sheen should disappear (with flat paint).

When covering a large area, start the first coat at the bottom and work the spray pattern back and forth. Start and end each pass off the model to keep the paint from loading up at the point where you reverse direction. Each pass should overlap the previous one slightly. For the second coat, turn the surface 90 degrees and repeat the process, Fig. 13. This crisscross spray method will help ensure even coverage.

Strip down, clean, and inspect. Most airbrush problems stem from inadequate cleaning. Paint residue inside the paint control valve, siphon tube, or at the bottom of the paint bottle aggravates clogging and can ruin subsequent color applications. Imagine this horror story: tiny flecks of dried black paint, worked loose by the passage of fresh paint, spit all over that beautiful white Testarossa you're spraying. Aaaagh!

If you want your airbrush to work properly every time, clean it after every painting session. Let's go through a complete strip-down and cleaning of a typical single-action airbrush, Fig. 14.

Air nozzle

Air button

Paint nozzle

Compression seal

Body

Locknut

Retaining nut

Washer

Paint tip

Siphon tube

Paint bottle

Fig. 14. The anatomy of a single-action airbrush.

First, check the manual that came with your airbrush — each brand has a different method of disassembly. After every painting session, spray clean thinner through the tip until it removes most of the residual paint. Next, detach the paint bottle or cup and put it aside. Loosen the locknut on the tip and unthread the nozzle from the tip. Use a thinner-soaked cotton swab to bathe the inside and outside of both parts, Fig. 15, followed by a slender, thinner-soaked pipe cleaner. Careful

now; forcing the pipe cleaner could damage the fragile nozzle.

Hold each part up to a strong light and look inside — the surfaces should be shiny and clean. If you can see paint residue inside, unscrew the retaining nut inside the paint nozzle and remove the rubber or nylon compression washer, Fig. 16. Soak the metal parts in lacquer thinner for a few hours, Fig. 17, repeat the cleaning process, reinstall the washer, and reassemble.

Check the air nozzle, too. Sometimes

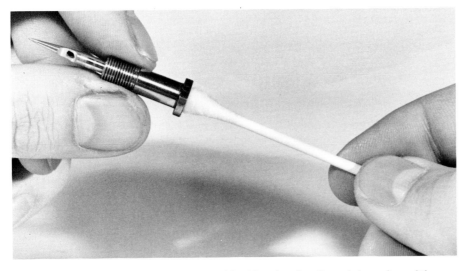

Fig. 15. Thinner-soaked cotton swabs are ideal for cleaning the paint nozzle and tip.

Fig. 16. Before soaking the paint valve to remove stubborn paint deposits, remove the compression seal — older ones made of rubber or vinyl could be destroyed by prolonged exposure to lacquer thinner.

Fig. 17. Soak the paint nozzle and tip in lacquer thinner, then repeat the cleaning process.

Fig. 18. A damaged paint nozzle (left) and bent paint tip will affect the airbrush's ability to paint fine lines. Replace them!

paint can splash up into the air nozzle guard and block the tiny hole.

Clean the paint bottle (or cup) and siphon tube with lacquer thinner and cotton swabs. The pipe cleaner should fit in most siphon tubes. Don't forget the outside of the bottle; spilled paint may get on your hands and then onto the model.

Inspect the nozzle and tip occasionally. A bent tip or cracked nozzle, Fig. 18, will cause the paint to spatter and you won't be able to achieve a fine line. Replacement tips and nozzles are usually sold together by dealers who sell airbrushes.

As I said at the beginning of this lesson, practice airbrushing. Experiment with different paints and thinning ratios. The more you practice, the more comfortable you'll feel and the more familiar you'll become with your airbrush's idiosyncrasies. Next time, we'll build on your new skills by airbrushing a model in a multicolor camouflage scheme. See you then. **FSM**

HOMEWORK ASSIGNMENT 7

Basic airbrushing

Materials: Single-action airbrush with air hose and paint bottle (or color cup), compressed gas source, model paint, thinner, lacquer thinner, mixing containers, old model to paint, cotton swabs, pipe cleaners

☐ Reread this lesson.
☐ Assemble materials next to your spray booth (you DO have one now, don't you?).
☐ Thin paint in separate container. Start with two parts paint to one part thinner. Mix thoroughly and pour into airbrush paint bottle.
☐ Turn on compressor and close airbrush paint nozzle.
☐ Depress air button and feel the air flow on your hand. Bring airbrush within ½" of your finger.
☐ Open paint nozzle and spray your old model 90 degrees to the surface. Start 3" away and move in to ½".
☐ Tilt model surface to 45 degrees and spray again. Try writing your name!
☐ Paint entire model one color with the crisscross method, then set aside to dry.
☐ Discard leftover thinned paint, or store separately from your fresh (unthinned) supply.
☐ Clean airbrush, being careful not to damage the tip.

This Focke-Wulf 190D looks as if it was photographed from the air by another pilot during World War Two. But it is a Revell 1/32 scale model, with airbrushed markings, built and photographed by Egbert Friedel of Moerendorf, West Germany.

Multicolor camouflage patterns can be applied freehand with an airbrush — it's the best tool for the job.

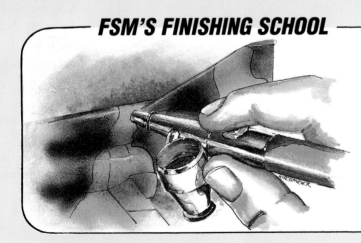

LESSON 8:

Advanced airbrushing

Mastering the master's tool

BY PAUL BOYER

NOW THAT YOU'VE painted and repainted just about every old model in your workshop, you're ready to create a masterpiece, right? Okay, I'll admit that like the construction of a certain large Mediterranean city state, mastering the airbrush is going to take time. A few of the techniques we'll cover in this lesson will help you speed things along, but practice is still the best teacher.

Before we begin, I'll assume you have a model that is assembled and ready to paint. I hope your airbrush is spotless, because spraying a multicolored scheme is not only going to test your ability, but will also test the capability of your airbrush.

Stop, look, and think. Before we start, let's look at the model you're about to paint and the multicolor scheme you've chosen. Do the colors on the real machine blend where they meet or is there a sharp demarcation line? If they do blend, are the lines diffuse or well defined? Are there corners or areas that will be difficult to paint? What about wheel wells or turret inte-

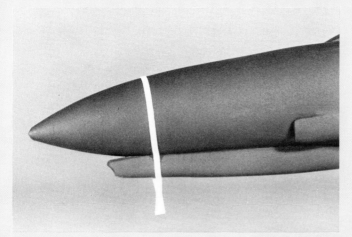

Fig. 1. Thin strips of tape make it easy to mask straight lines on curved surfaces.

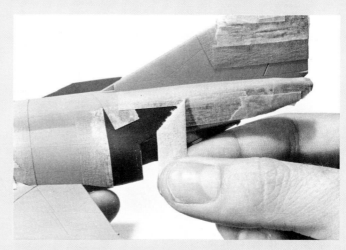

Fig. 2. When removing masking tape, pull it over itself at a 90-degree angle from the color demarcation line.

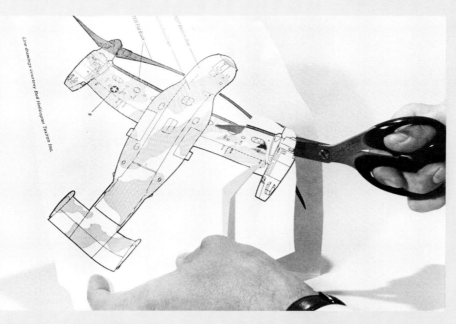

Fig. 3. Blow up camouflage patterns to the scale of your model and cut them out.

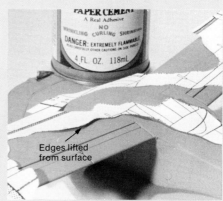

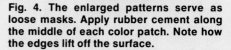

Edges lifted from surface

Fig. 4. The enlarged patterns serve as loose masks. Apply rubber cement along the middle of each color patch. Note how the edges lift off the surface.

riors? Will you need to mask them before airbrushing? What about canopies? Hmmm. Not as ready as you thought you were, are you?

Camouflage. One of the reasons modelers paint with an airbrush is to faithfully reproduce blended multicolor camouflage schemes — it's the best tool for the job. In real life, military equipment is painted at the manufacturing plant, repair depot, or in the field. A technician is handed a spray gun, cans of paint, a pattern, and told to "paint that tank, soldier."

So, what are we doing? Pretty much the same thing, only on a smaller scale. When airbrushing camouflage, thin two parts of paint with one part of thinner. You may find that you'll need to thin the paint even more, especially Polly S acrylics. Your goal is to make the airbrush paint the thinnest line possible without clogging.

The logical progression in painting

multicolor camouflage schemes is to first paint the entire model with the lightest camouflage color. Why? Well, the light color serves as a primer, and it's easier to cover a light color with a darker one. The light primer makes it easier to see surface flaws. After you've corrected the flaws, spray and check again.

The next color to go on is the next darkest. To prevent the second color from reacting with the first, wait until the first color is completely dry. Depending on what type of paint you use, the wait could be a few hours to a few days.

Masking techniques for sharp lines. There are three types of color demarcation lines found in camouflage: sharp lines, tight blended lines, and soft blended lines. You'll need masks when you airbrush one of the first two types, and I'll discuss a couple masking techniques.

When the color demarcation lines are sharp, use tape if the lines are straight or a liquid masking agent if the pattern is irregular. Cutting tape into thin strips makes it easier to mask straight lines around curved surfaces, Fig. 1. Make sure the edges of the tape are burnished down to the surface of the model to keep the line sharp. Spray as soon as you can after applying the tape — as time goes on, the tape will tend to lift, allowing overspray to creep underneath, creating soft spots in the line.

Concentrate on what you are painting. It's easy to get mixed up when applying a mask. Check to make sure you are covering the area you want to protect, not the area you want to paint.

Remove the mask as soon as the paint is dry to the touch. Carefully pull the tape back over itself 90 degrees to the demarcation line, Fig. 2. Lifting the tape straight up from the surface runs the risk of lifting the first color.

Tight blended lines. If the demarcation lines on the original vehicle are tight, but still obviously blended, I'll airbrush the model using a technique I

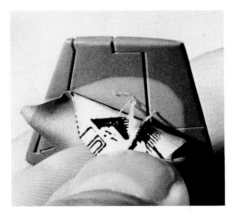

Fig. 5. After airbrushing the next camouflage color, remove the loose masks.

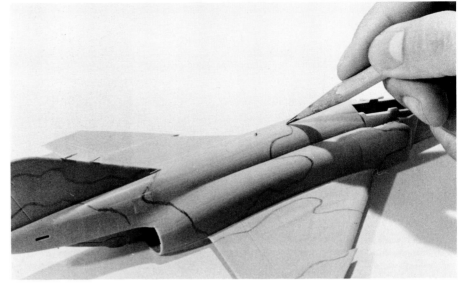

Fig. 6. It's easier to follow pencil lines on the model when airbrushing complex camouflage patterns freehand.

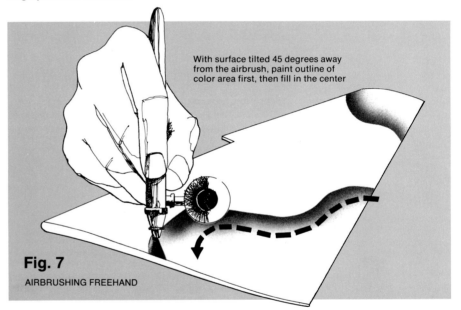

With surface tilted 45 degrees away from the airbrush, paint outline of color area first, then fill in the center

Fig. 7

AIRBRUSHING FREEHAND

call "loose masking." Although it can be time-consuming, loose masking produces beautiful results.

Using an enlarging/reducing copier, make several copies of the camouflage pattern in the same scale as the model. Cut out the areas of the first (lightest) color you've already applied, Fig. 3. Now, stick these paper patterns onto the model with dabs of rubber cement, Fig. 4. Don't worry whether the edges fit tight to the model — they shouldn't. With the edges of the paper masks lifted slightly off the surface of the model, the airbrush produces a tight (but not sharp) color demarcation line, Fig. 5.

Spray perpendicular to the surface of the model — spraying into the mask will lift the paper and create too soft a line; spraying away from the mask may create too sharp a line.

When finished with the second color, cut out the masks for that color, apply them to the model, and repeat the process.

Soft blended lines. For simple patterns and wide blended demarcation lines, freehand spraying works well. If the color patterns are more complex, I'll lightly draw the patterns on the first color with a pencil, Fig. 6, then paint over the lines.

Freehand airbrushing takes practice. You'll have to eyeball where each color goes, constantly checking reference diagrams or photos. Use thin paint, a lot of air pressure (30 psi is ideal), and set the paint nozzle to produce the thinnest line possible.

When airbrushing freehand, paint the edges of each patch of color first, Fig. 7. Hold the model so the surface you're painting is tilted 45 degrees away from the airbrush, Fig. 8. Remember your experiments in our last lesson? Spraying at an angle produces a tighter line at the bottom of the spray pattern, softer at the top. Turning and twisting the model, you'll be able to keep the pattern moving around the color demarcation line. After you've

drawn the edges of each patch, go back and fill in the centers.

Be careful, though, on corners. As you spray to an edge, sight along the airbrush and observe what is behind the area you are spraying. Let's say you're airbrushing over the top of the fuselage of a Phantom. As you come over the top, watch out! There's a wing out there that's going to receive overspray, Fig. 9. Selected masking will help prevent little setbacks like this.

You're bound to make mistakes no matter which method you use. Although time-consuming, you can always go back and retouch with the other colors. But before you start retouching, clean the airbrush — you don't want some of that dark green ruining your desert sand! Just as you did when you painted the model, start with the lightest color, then go to the darker colors. You may find yourself

retouching a couple of times before the model is painted to your satisfaction.

Masking canopies. Perhaps the most difficult area to paint on aircraft models is the canopy. It's small, fragile, and easily messed up. My favorite method of masking around canopy frames is with Scotch Magic tape (the frosty kind).

First, apply a piece of tape to each side or facet of the canopy. Burnish the tape down with a fingernail or a balsa stick. See how the tape highlights the canopy frame lines? They show white and are easy to see. Now with a brand new No. 11 modeling knife blade and a steady hand, carefully cut the tape from corner to corner around each pane. Repeat the procedure until every pane is finished, then carefully lift the tape from the framing with tweezers, Fig. 10. Make sure that the edges of the tape on the panes are tight. If you're painting the canopy before installing it on the model, make sure you cover the *inside* with tape.

Remove the tape from the canopy as soon as the paint is dry to the touch. If you leave the tape on for more than a couple of days, the adhesive may bond to the plastic better than it does to the tape. If this happens, repeatedly press and lift fresh tape to remove the residue.

Here's a tip: Canopy framing is usually painted black, medium gray, or interior green on the inside. Don't try to mask and paint the framing on the inside of the canopy, though. Simply apply the inside framing color to the outside of the masked canopy first, then follow with the outside color. You'll be able to see the inside color through the clear plastic, Fig. 11. Neat, huh?

I know what you're thinking: "He's going to tell us to practice again." You're right! No amount of lecturing on any modeling technique will help unless you practice. The more you use your airbrush, the better your results will be. Besides, you'll need to sharpen up for our next lesson: natural-metal finishes. Oooh! **FSM**

END LESSON 8

HOMEWORK ASSIGNMENT 8
Advanced airbrushing

Materials: Single-action airbrush with air hose and paint bottle (or color cup), compressed gas source, model paint, thinner, lacquer thinner, mixing containers, old model to paint, cotton swabs, pipe cleaners, masking tape, Scotch Magic tape, sharp blade, rubber cement, pencil

☐ Reread this lesson.
☐ Choose the technique above which will produce the kind of color demarcation line you need.
☐ Mask over cockpits, landing gear wells, interiors, canopies, and other areas that should not be painted.
☐ Thin two parts of camouflage paint to one part compatible thinner.
☐ Airbrush lightest camouflage color over entire model.
☐ Inspect for surface blemishes, correct them, and respray.
☐ Apply the next darkest camouflage color freehand or with masks over the areas to remain the first color.
☐ Airbrush the remaining camouflage colors, working from light to dark.
☐ Clean the airbrush thoroughly.
☐ Retouch if necessary, starting with the lightest color.

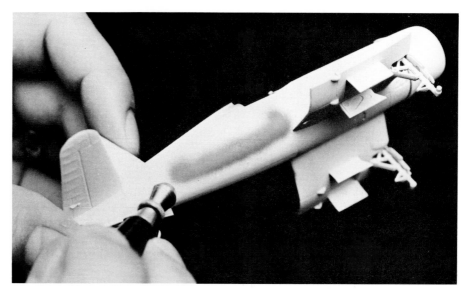

Fig. 8. When airbrushing color demarcation lines freehand, tilt the surface of the model back 45 degrees so that the tight portion of the spray pattern forms the line.

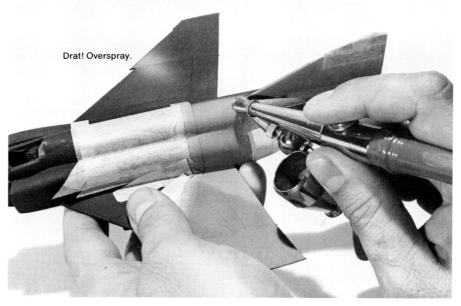

Drat! Overspray.

Fig. 9. Oops! Should have masked that wing. When applying camouflage, whether freehand or with masks, make sure that the parts of the model behind the area you're spraying are protected.

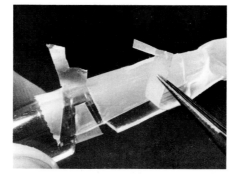

Fig. 10. Paul's favorite canopy masking material is Scotch Magic tape. Cut the tape on the canopy with a sharp blade, then remove the tape from the frames.

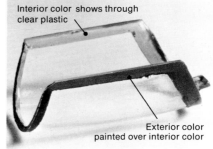

Interior color shows through clear plastic

Exterior color painted over interior color

Fig. 11. Canopy trick. Apply the interior canopy frame color on the exterior first, then cover it with the exterior color. You'll be able to see the interior color inside the canopy.

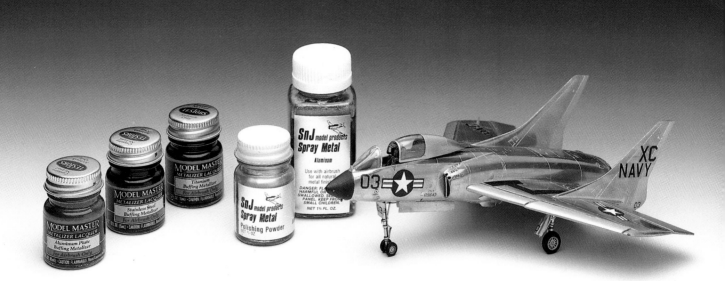

Buffable metallic paints can make a plastic model look like it was made of metal. Ross Whitaker built this natural metal 1/72 scale Fujimi F7U-3 Cutlass.

LESSON 9:
Natural metal finishes

Difficult, yet spectacular

Paul's F-101A Voodoo fighter was converted from a 1/72 scale Hasegawa RF-101C reconnaissance version and painted with Testor Metalizer.

BY PAUL BOYER

NOW THAT YOU'RE all masters of the airbrush, you're ready to tackle one of the most difficult model aircraft finishes: unpainted metal. For years, modelers have struggled with silver enamels, aluminum lacquers, foils, and buffable metallics, and I've tried them all. Although I still use each of these for certain effects, for overall natural metal finishes I prefer buffable metallic paints.

The first of these airbrushable metal finishes appeared in the early 1970s. Back then, both Liqu-a-plate and Spray 'n' Plate offered a new paint technology — extremely fine-grained aluminum pigment that could be airbrushed without thinning, then buffed with a soft cloth to a realistic unpainted metal finish. The advantage of these paints was obvious: a real metal look with relatively little work. Unfortunately, buffable metallics produce fragile finishes.

Paul's 1/72 scale Hasegawa P-47D Razorback was painted with SnJ Spray Metal.

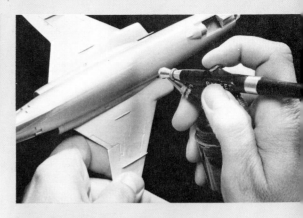

Fig. 2. Spray on three or four light, misty coats of buffable metallic paint.

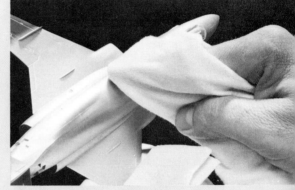

Fig. 3. After waiting a few minutes for the paint to dry, start buffing with a soft cloth. Make sure you handle the model with a gloved hand or with another cloth.

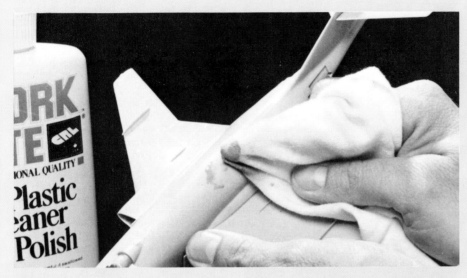

Fig. 1. The key to a brilliant natural metal finish with buffable metallics is a glass-smooth surface. Start with careful assembly and minimum use of filler putty. Plastic polish is available from plastic supply stores; hobby shops often stock it, too.

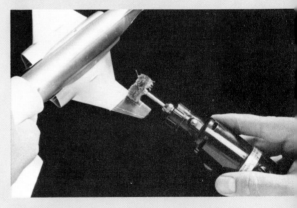

Fig. 4. Using a rag wheel on a motor tool can speed the buffing process, but it takes practice.

Handling and masking can remove the aluminum particles which cling tenuously to the plastic surface.

Newcomers. Neither Liqu-a-plate nor Spray 'n' Plate is manufactured today, but a similar product, Metalizer, was produced in the early 1980s and has since been adopted into the Testor Model Master line. Metalizer includes a number of shades to simulate the different alloys used on modern aircraft. Similar in concept to the earlier buffable metallics, Metalizer also requires special handling and masking techniques.

Yet another buffable metallic is available — SnJ Spray Metal. This product is similar to the others, but features a sturdier finish and aluminum powder which can be buffed into the already-painted surface for extra shine.

Surface preparation. No matter whether you use enamel, lacquer, foil, or buffable metallics, the surface to be finished in natural metal must be flawless. Why? Silver and aluminum fin-

ishes highlight every scratch, pit, and ripple, so arm yourself with fine sandpaper, plastic polish, and a sharp eye.

The best way to avoid surface flaws is not to create them during assembly. Since the buffable metallic paints depend on a smooth surface to look best, avoid extensive use of fillers. Most fillers are more porous than styrene and tend to soak up metallics. To avoid fillers, make the most of your time fitting the parts of the kit together — extra care in assembly will create a smoother surface for the paint.

If you must fill and sand surface imperfections, here's what to do. First even off the surface with 400-grit wet-or-dry sandpaper, used wet — the water helps the sanding dust flow away from the work and keeps the sandpaper from clogging. Wash away the remaining sludge and examine the sanded area. If any seams or pits need to be refilled, do it now, then sand again. My favorite filler is gap-filling super

glue, set quickly with an accelerator.

Next, sand the area with 600-grit wet-or-dry sandpaper and water. This fine-grit sandpaper smooths out the imperfections and reduces the scratches made by the 400-grit paper.

Incidentally, with metallic finishes we won't be priming the model before applying the finish coats. Primer is usually a flat white or gray paint, and its surface isn't nearly as smooth as polished plastic.

Polish. After sanding, the next step

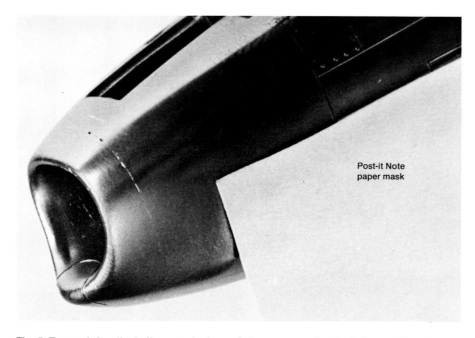

Fig. 5. To mask for dissimilar panels, Larry Schramm uses low-tack tape or Post-it note papers. Only about 1/16" of the tape or paper is exposed, reducing the amount of metallic paint that could lift off.

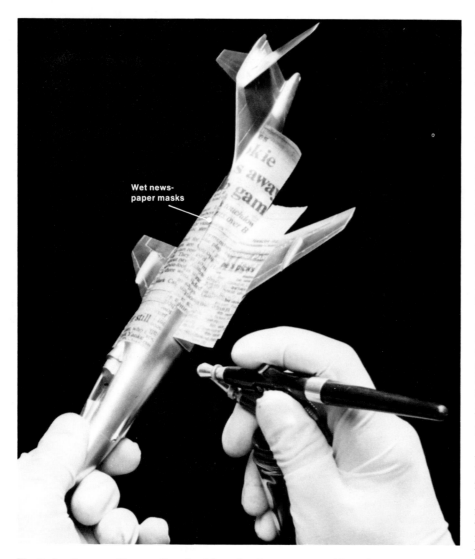

Fig. 6. Another masking medium is strips of wet newspaper, although masking around small panels this way is a chore.

is to polish the surface of the entire model. Available from a plastic supply house, plastic polish is a fine liquid compound which can produce a glass-like surface on styrene — just what we need for buffable metallics. Other products that polish plastic well are Blue Magic metal polish (you can find it in auto supply stores) and Brasso, although you may find its ammonia content irritating.

Pour a dab of plastic polish on a soft rag (an old T-shirt is ideal), and apply it to the surface of the model, Fig. 1. Rub with a circular motion and work a small area at a time. As you rub, the liquid starts to dry, leaving a light film on the surface. You'll also notice that the polish leaves a residue in indentations. Keep rubbing until the film starts to reveal the bare plastic below. Keep rubbing. As you continue, the plastic becomes shinier. You may have to reapply polish and repeat the process a few times, but your goal is a glass-like surface. So keep rubbing.

Once you've got that beautiful shiny surface, wash the model with soap and water and a toothbrush. Concentrate on removing the residue from recessed panel lines, hinge lines, and corners. Dry the model with a hair dryer set on medium heat and handle the model with surgical gloves — fingerprints on the plastic may repel the metallic paint.

Spray. Buffable metallic paints normally don't require thinning, but both Testor and SnJ have special thinners available for their paints should they thicken with age. Shake the paint bottle vigorously so that the metal pigment is mixed thoroughly with the vehicle (the liquid part of the paint). Since there is no thinning, I usually empty the bottle into the airbrush bottle. As you airbrush, you'll need to stir the paint in the airbrush bottle occasionally to keep the metal pigment in suspension.

Buffable metallics come in different shades, including steel, magnesium, titanium, burnt metal, and others to simulate the various metals used in aircraft and automobile construction. Since most of an aircraft's skin is aluminum, I always spray the entire model with the aluminum shade first. We'll get to applying the other shades later.

Spray light, misty coats — you don't want the paint to go on wet or puddle. You'll need several passes to cover sufficiently, Fig. 2.

After letting the paint dry for a few minutes, you can start the transformation to a brilliant polished finish. Using a clean cotton T-shirt or diaper (the reusable kind; remember those?), begin to buff the paint, Fig. 3. Go lightly at first, gradually increasing pressure as

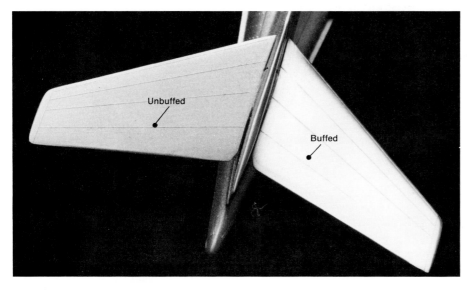

Fig. 7. Leaving a few panels unbuffed also produces a dissimilar panel effect. Here, the right elevator has been buffed.

Fig. 8. Bare-Metal Foil is great for chrome trim on auto and truck models.

you rub. Note how the paint becomes more and more shiny. Keep rubbing. Soon the painted plastic looks like unpainted metal. It's easier to establish this effect on curved surfaces — flat surfaces take more buffing. If you buff right down to the plastic, don't panic. Simply respray and buff again.

If rubbing is too tedious for you, you can buff the paint with a cotton rag wheel in a motor tool, Fig. 4, but be careful. Use a slow speed and work gradually — it's easy to buff right through the paint with this tool.

Masking. Due to the fragile nature of the finish, masking over buffable metallics should be kept to a minimum. One of the masters of metallic finishes, Larry Schramm, uses low-tack tape such as Scotch Removable tape (in the blue plaid container) and Post-it note papers, which also have a low-tack adhesive. He only uses about 1/16" of the tape or paper to form the masked line and covers the rest of the metal-painted area with paper or plastic wrap, Fig. 5.

The best solution is to paint the other colors before applying the metallics. This presents a problem. Since the buffable metallics work best on bare

plastic, you'll need to carefully mask the plastic *around* the area to be painted, spray, then when dry, mask *over* the painted area before applying the metallics.

Dissimilar panels. One of the advantages of buffable metallics is that you can simulate different types of metal. Testor Metalizer comes in eight buffable shades plus five non-buffing shades, while SnJ Spray Metal offers four colors. By studying reference books and photos of the subject you're modeling, you can determine the approximate shade of each panel. After the model is painted overall aluminum, you can carefully mask around panels and spray on a different shade. You can add different shades before or after buffing the base aluminum coat.

Testor recommends masking with wet newspaper — now there's something completely different! Simply cut strips of newspaper, moisten them with water, and lay them down along the panel lines, Fig. 6. Soak up excess water with a cloth, make final adjustments, spray on the new shade, and lift the paper. Most shades (except for the dark ones such as Exhaust) can be buffed after removing the paper masks

and won't "bleed" onto adjacent panels.

You can also simulate dissimilar panels by how much you buff the paint. A shiny, highly buffed panel next to one that has not been buffed certainly will look different, Fig. 7.

Overcoats. Although the manufacturers of buffable metallics produce clear overcoats called "sealers," I don't use them. I find that they reduce the natural metal effect, making the model look like it has been painted with glossy silver paint. However, sealers allow you to handle the model after it has been painted, so you could compromise by spraying sealer over the areas where you expect to touch the model.

Foils. Bare-Metal Foil is a self-adhesive aluminum alloy foil that is thin enough to reveal all surface details. Although you could cover an entire model with foil for a realistic finish, I find it tedious. However, nothing beats Bare-Metal Foil for chrome trim on car and truck models.

Cut the foil with a sharp knife and peel it away from its backing paper. After laying the foil onto the surface, you can burnish it down with a soft cloth over your fingernail. Now all you have to do is cut around the area with a sharp blade, lift away the excess foil, Fig. 8, and burnish again to remove leftover adhesive. I often use Bare-Metal Foil for the oleo portions of landing gear struts.

You won't need to apply a clear gloss over buffable metallics or foil before decaling. The surface is smooth enough to prevent the dreaded "silvering." We'll discuss more about this problem, and the decaling techniques we can use to prevent it, in our next lesson. **FSM**

END LESSON 9

HOMEWORK ASSIGNMENT 9
Natural metal finishes

Materials: Airbrush, model, plastic polish, toothbrush, buffable metallic paints, soft cloth, low-tack tape, latex or cotton gloves

☐ Reread this lesson.
☐ Polish model with plastic polish.
☐ Examine the model for flaws, fix them, and repolish.
☐ Wash model with soapy water and dry with hair dryer.
☐ Spray on three or four misty coats of metallic paint.
☐ After waiting a few minutes, buff paint with a soft cloth.
☐ Choose masking method and apply dissimilar panels with alternate shades of metallic paint.
☐ Buff new panels.

Decaling can be a delight or a disaster. When everything works right, markings are often the highlight of a model. Paul works on a 1/72 scale Hasegawa F-4J Phantom.

FSM'S FINISHING SCHOOL

LESSON 10:

Applying decals

Decals will make or
break a beautiful model

BY PAUL BOYER

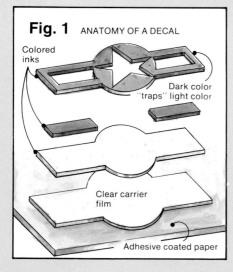

Fig. 1 ANATOMY OF A DECAL

Colored inks

Dark color "traps" light color

Clear carrier film

Adhesive coated paper

UNLIKE MOST of the other things you have learned during this course, decaling isn't new to you — you probably applied decals to every model you have ever made. Even back when you were a little kid, you stuck those wet, slimy things on your models. Sure, they didn't stay on long, and they weren't in the right positions, but hey, decaling is easy, right? You're not smiling.

Okay, I'll admit decaling is not as easy as it appears. A lot of things can go wrong (and probably will) while decaling. Decals can curl up or come apart, ink can bleed, adhesive may not stick — or stick where you don't want it

to — markings may not fit, or could be the wrong size or the wrong color . . . you get the picture.

What is a decal? Most model decals are water-slide (or wet-transfer), but nowadays you can also find after-market dry-transfer (or rub-on) decals. For this lesson, we'll stick (whew!) with conventional water-slide decals.

A decal is a thin, flexible sandwich of inks and carrier film that is printed on paper which has a water-soluble adhesive coating. In most cases, the clear carrier film is the first thing to be printed on the paper. This film is sometimes applied over the entire sheet, but more often it is "spot" printed only where colored inks will go on top of it.

Fig. 2. Many decals printed by lithography are translucent and allow the colors of the painted model to show through.

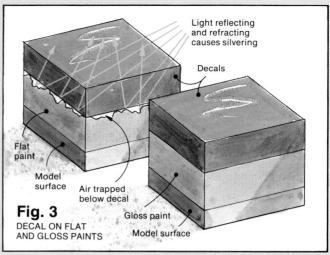

Light reflecting and refracting causes silvering

Decals

Flat paint

Model surface

Air trapped below decal

Gloss paint

Model surface

Fig. 3
DECAL ON FLAT AND GLOSS PAINTS

Fig. 5. First, make sure the model has a smooth gloss surface. If not painted with gloss paints, apply a clear gloss overcoat to flat paint.

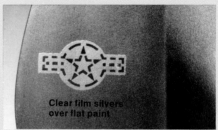

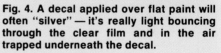

Clear film silvers over flat paint

Fig. 4. A decal applied over flat paint will often "silver" — it's really light bouncing through the clear film and in the air trapped underneath the decal.

Next come the colors, usually starting with the lightest. White often underlies other light colors to increase their opacity and brilliance. The remaining colors follow, sometimes "trapping" colors beneath them to create the proper image, Fig. 1.

Most high-quality water-slide decals are printed by a silk-screen press via a photographic process. Some kit manufacturers have their decals printed by lithography — it's quicker and cheaper, but sometimes the decals are more difficult to apply due to the stiffer inks and carriers used. Unfortunately, these decals aren't as opaque as they should be — light colors allow the color of the model to show through, Fig. 2.

When dipped in water, the water-soluble adhesive dissolves and releases the film/ink sandwich from the paper. Some of the adhesive remains on the underside of the carrier film and this is what sticks the decal to the model.

Decal problems. Most decal problems fall into three categories: sticking, silvering, and conforming to irregular surfaces. The first two, sticking and silvering, can be solved for the most part by ensuring that the decals are applied to a smooth, glossy surface. "Oh, no," you cry, because you've just painted your model with flat paints. Now what?

Many modeling paints come in a flat finish — they cover better and dry quicker than gloss paints, but that isn't helping us now. If you could look at flat paint under a microscope, you would see a surface resembling sandpaper — tiny peaks and valleys. Glossy paint, on the other hand, has a smooth, level surface. Now, how does the surface affect decal adhesion? Any guesses? Well, although the decal is flexible, it's not flexible enough to conform to all those peaks and valleys, much like laying a piece of glass on coarse sandpaper. The decal makes contact only with the tops of the peaks; not much surface to cling

to, Fig. 3. On a gloss surface, though, the decal comes in contact with the entire surface, and sticks.

The other problem with decals applied over flat paints is "silvering." This is caused by light refracting and reflecting in the air trapped in the valleys of the flat paint under the decal. Let's look through our microscope again. Light travels through the clear film areas of the decal, through the air trapped underneath, bounces off the valleys, through the air again, and up through the clear film. Anytime light travels through different mediums it bends (refracts). This, and the scattered reflections off the uneven surface of the flat paint, causes an opalescent appearance we call silvering, Fig. 4. Looks awful, doesn't it?

Okay, now how do we get rid of silvering? Use gloss paints. Yes, but what if you can't find gloss paints for the colors you need? Ahah! Someone suggested a clear gloss overcoat. Right. Many clear gloss coatings are produced and all of them will work, but you'll need to be careful that the gloss you apply doesn't react with the colored paints below.

My favorite clear gloss is Floquil's Crystal-Cote; it's water-clear and quick drying, but its formula can dissolve most modeling paints if applied incorrectly. I dust on a few coats and gradu-

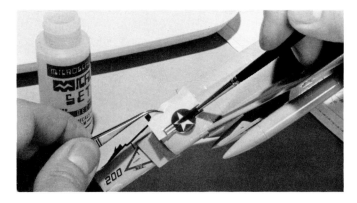

Fig. 7. Applying decal solvent to the model before you add the decal will help reduce air bubbles underneath the decal.

Fig. 8. Carefully slide the decal onto the model with the brush while holding the backing paper with tweezers.

AFTER SCHOOL

It's time to answer some questions you've had about previous FSM Finishing School lessons. Who's first?

"Mark Stearns, Murphysboro, Illinois. I'm having a problem with the 3M Blenderm tape you recommended in Lesson 2. I find it leaves some of the adhesive behind and I have to remove it with solvent. I've had better luck with Pactra masking tape available in hobby shops. It doesn't leave residue and is less expensive than Blenderm."

Thanks for the tip, Mark. Yes, Blenderm can leave adhesive behind, especially if the tape is left on the model for a while. This is also a problem with Scotch Magic Mending tape (green plaid) and certain other tapes as well. I remove the adhesive by pressing a fresh piece of tape onto the residue and lifting it off. This may have to be repeated a number of times, but I think it is less messy than using a solvent. I'll have to try the Pactra tape you mentioned.

"John Howard, Fairfax, Virginia. In Lesson 4 you recommended throwing a couple beebees into each bottle of paint to serve as agitators. That's a fine idea, but beebees will rust in water-based paints such as Polly S and Pactra Acrylic. I know; I've ruined a few bottles. Instead of beebees, I drop in a couple of stainless-steel machine-screw nuts (¼" x 20NC) — they won't rust."

Even the old teacher can learn new tricks. Yes, beebees can rust in water-based paints. I checked back in a few bottles and found them slowly corroding. Substituting stainless-steel nuts is an excellent idea. Thanks.

"Brian Yocum, Hastings, Nebraska. Going back to Lesson 1, I have trouble with the dispenser tips for super glues. Every one I've tried clogs. What's your secret?"

Well, Brian, the secret is not to use those fine tips. I've never found one that doesn't clog, either. I buy the smallest bottle of glue available — a small bottle will last me a year and super glue tends to thicken and eventually solidify. I cut off the tip of the bottle and squeeze a drop or two onto a scrap of sheet styrene or aluminum foil. Then I transfer small drops of the glue to the model with a toothpick.

"Jason Boden, Massapequa Park, New York. In Lesson 2, you suggested airbrushing Floquil Primer directly onto plastic. I've always heard that Floquil attacks styrene and that you should use Floquil Barrier before applying any Floquil paint. Can you explain this apparent contradiction?"

I'll try, Jason. Yes, Floquil paints attack styrene — the vehicle contains xylene and other solvents that can dissolve styrene. However, if airbrushed lightly, the vehicle dries within a few seconds and the paint just "bites" the plastic surface a little. However, if you should flood Floquil on or attempt to hand brush it, these heavy applications would allow more time for the solvents to react with the plastic. Barrier is a precautionary measure, but I've never used it. Just go slowly and you shouldn't have problems.

"Dave Tirschman, Baltimore, Maryland. Ross Martinek's contribution in Lesson 6 left me with both a lot of information and a question. Would I still need a spray booth if I airbrush only acrylic paints?"

As Ross indicated in his article, what is considered harmless today may be found deadly tomorrow. I suggest you use a spray booth every time you paint, no matter what type of paint you use. It's not easy putting one together and finding a place for it, but health doesn't come cheap.

Paul Boyer

ally build up a gloss surface. If you spray it on too quickly or too wet, it can ruin the paint underneath. Try to stay away from any clear coat that is yellowish in the bottle. I've found that they tend to yellow even more with age, altering the color of the model.

Wait! You wanted your model to have a flat finish. What is the next step after decaling? Right again! Spray on a clear *flat* overcoat. This restores the scale appearance of the finish, and as a bonus, seals the decals to the paint. If you want a gloss finish, simply spray

Fig. 6. Lightly cut through the clear film around the image area. Pressing too hard may crack the colored inks.

Fig. 9. Sighting along those long, straight decals will help you see kinks and bends.

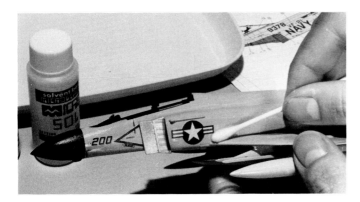

Fig. 10. Soak up excess water with a cotton swab. Just touch the corner and the water will wick away.

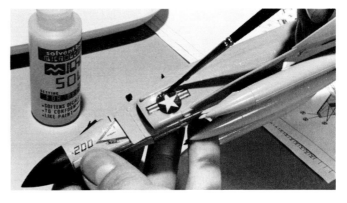

Fig. 11. Decal solvent applied over the decal will soften the film and allow the decal to conform to surface detail.

another coat of clear gloss over the decals.

Some decals won't stick properly, even to a glossy surface. Why? Perhaps the water-base adhesive on the decal paper is inadequate, causing the edges of the decal to lift from the surface. When this happens, I dilute white glue with water and decal solvent and brush it underneath the lifted edges. I may have to "ride herd" on the decal and keep prodding the edges down as the glue takes effect.

Now let's tackle the third problem, making decals conform to surface irregularities. To make decals more flexible, a decal solvent can be applied. Decal solvents (also called setting solutions) come in many formulas. They are designed to soften the clear carrier film and inks (without dissolving them) and allow the decal to snuggle down over surface details. A few decal solvents are so strong they can literally destroy certain decals — they can even dissolve some modeling paints. Experiment on an insignificant decal before working on your model; I often sacrifice an underside stencil or marking option to test a new solvent.

All these measures are designed to make the decals look as though they have been painted on the surface of the model. Now that we know the princi-

ples involved, let's go through decaling step by step.

Apply gloss. If your model has been painted with flat paints, and if there are a lot of decals to apply, spray a clear gloss coat over the entire model, Fig. 5. It's easier to give the model an overall coat than to spray each area separately. Allow the clear gloss to dry thoroughly — a tacky gloss coat will pick up fingerprints easily. The gloss doesn't have to be glass smooth, but you should be able to see light reflect from the model — that's good enough for decaling.

Assemble your tools. You'll need the following for decaling your model: small sharp scissors, sharp No. 11 blade, a good-quality brush, tweezers (the ones made for stamp collectors are best), shallow pan of warm water, decal solvent, soft absorbent cloth, and for emergencies, white glue.

Before we begin, let's discuss what to do with clear carrier film. There are two schools of thought here. Some modelers cut away as much clear film as possible, while others believe that the soft edges of the spot-printed clear film are less obtrusive than fresh-cut edges. Cutting away the clear film is time-consuming, but it's a good idea when using thick decals. I go with either method, but I always cut away clear

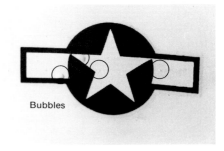

Fig. 12. Occasionally, air bubbles will be trapped underneath the decal. Simply lance them with a sharp blade and apply a little more decal solvent.

film from decals going on natural-metal-finished models.

If you decide to cut away the extra clear film, use a sharp blade and just a little pressure, Fig. 6. You shouldn't be cutting through the paper — that much force may bend the edge of the image areas of the decal and cause the inks to crack and crumble away once dipped in water. Properly cut, excess film will separate from the image when the decal is soaked.

One, two, three, dip! Work on one side of the model at a time and try to keep the side you're working on horizontal. This will keep water and decal solvent where you want them and the

Fig. 13. It's important to wipe up the residue from decal adhesive and decal solvents.

Fig. 14. A coat of clear gloss or clear flat will seal the decals and provide a uniform sheen.

It's hard not to be impressed with the intricate detail of this Italian kit Chinese junk. Built by Arthur Gehring of Fort Washington, Pennsylvania, the boat was dressed with Floquil Swedish wood oil and finished with Floquil gloss. Photo by Paul Hertel.

decal from shifting out of position. Cut out one decal at a time, carefully noting its position by studying the instruction sheet.

Dip the decal in warm (not hot) water for a few seconds until the backing paper is soaked. Lay the wet decal and paper on a paper towel or absorbent cloth. Pick up the decal and backing with the tweezer and place it next to the spot where it goes on the model. Try not to handle the decal — wet decals will stick to your fingers, too. Using the brush, apply a few drops of decal solvent to the model, Fig. 7 — this will serve as a wetting agent, reducing the chance of air bubbles forming underneath the decal.

Now, carefully push the decal off the backing paper with the brush and slide it into position, Fig. 8. This stage is especially tricky with large and long decals — use plenty of water to keep the decal loose while you adjust its position. Take your time. You'll be able to see kinks and bends in those long, straight decals by sighting along the model, Fig. 9.

Once you have the decal in position, soak up excess water with a soft cloth or cotton swab, Fig. 10; just touch it to the corner of the decal and let the water wick away.

Snuggle with solvent. Now apply a few drops of decal solvent with the brush, Fig. 11. Brush over the entire decal, making sure the solvent goes over the edges. Allow the solvent to soften the decal for a few minutes, then wick away excess solvent with a swab. It's extremely important not to touch or try to move the decal at this stage. The decal becomes so soft it will stretch and distort if disturbed. Don't try to squash the decal onto the model's surface — you may find the decal stubbornly attached to your finger or cloth. Let the solvent work its magic. After a few minutes, the decal will start to look lumpy or wrinkled. As long as the solvent isn't too strong for the decal, this is a natural effect. Soon, the solvent begins to dry and the film starts to snuggle down onto the surface.

You can work assembly-line fashion by applying the decals from one end of the model to the other, going back to soak up extra water or applying solvent as you wait for the next decal to soak. Before flipping the model over to work on another side, make sure the decals are dry. Solvent-softened decals are easily damaged.

Clean up. After the decals have dried, go back and inspect them for bubbles, Fig. 12. If you find them, lance each with a sharp knife and apply a small drop of setting solution. The bubble should deflate and disappear as the solution dries.

Look closely at the decaled areas and you may see residue from the decal adhesive, solvent, and water. Wet a cotton swab or cloth with warm water and mop up the stains, Fig. 13. This is important since some decal adhesives turn rusty after a few months. If water doesn't loosen the residue, try decal solvent.

Overcoat. Now, you'll need to decide what final finish you want on your model. Flat? Gloss? Something in between? A clear overcoat not only produces the finish you want, but it also seals the decals on the model, Fig. 14. Some aircraft have a flat finish on top, glossy below.

As with the clear gloss undercoat, you should determine which overcoat will be compatible with your paint, but now you have the additional concern of how the overcoat will affect the decals. For a flat overcoat, I prefer Pactra Acrylic clear flat — it has a nice semigloss sheen that's not too flat, not too shiny.

Now you should have a clean, beautiful model. But what if you don't want it so clean? What about a little scale dirt and grease? Next time, we'll talk about weathering techniques. See you then.

FSM

END LESSON 10

HOMEWORK ASSIGNMENT 10
Dealing with decals

Materials: Painted model, decals, shallow dish of warm water, decal solvent, scissors, sharp knife, tweezers, brush, cotton swabs, soft absorbent cloth, clear gloss paint, clear flat paint, white glue.

☐ Reread this lesson.
☐ If painted with flat paints, overcoat the model with clear gloss.
☐ Cut out each decal image individually.
☐ Dip decal in water until paper is soaked.
☐ As you wait for decal to loosen from paper, apply a few drops of decal solvent to the area to receive the decal.
☐ Place decal next to the area it goes on the model.
☐ Push the decal off the paper and into position.
☐ Absorb excess water with cloth or swab.
☐ Apply decal solvent over the decal.
☐ After a few minutes, wick away excess solvent.
☐ When dry, inspect for bubbles, lance them, and apply more solvent.
☐ Mop up adhesive, solvent, and water stains.
☐ Overcoat with clear gloss or clear flat.

A dusting of pastels is the finishing touch on this 1/35 scale Italeri M109 self-propelled howitzer. Note the stains on hinges, bolts, and exhaust pipe.

LESSON 11:

Basic weathering

Subtle shading and highlighting enhance realism

BY PAUL BOYER

ALL RIGHT, what separates a spectacular model from a field of ho-hum models? Finish helps, yes, and that's what this school is all about. But what is that little extra something that makes certain models eye-catching? Paint and decals don't always make the difference. There is something more. *Realism!* Models which look so real that photos of them look like photos of the real thing!

"Factory fresh" models are pretty, but they're not necessarily realistic. Most models are small-scale replicas of machines, and machines either move or have moving parts. Motion and moving parts mean friction and lubrication, fuel and exhaust, wear and tear, and eventually decay and abandonment. All these characteristics can be applied to the finish of your model.

What is weathering? Modelers use the term "weathering" for everything from exhaust stains to mud splatters. Well, what else can we call it — "dirtying"? Yech! So weathering a model not only replicates the effects of weather, but also the effects of normal operation.

Before you begin weathering, look at photos of the actual machine you are modeling. In most cases, automobiles are clean, but tanks are dirty. Aircraft and ships usually fall somewhere in between.

Let's take a look at aircraft. Except for those that just rolled out of the paint shop, aircraft show at least a little weathering. Oil, grease, and fuel stain the finish and streak across the surface when blown by the air rushing over the aircraft's surface. The same goes for powder stains from weapons and exhaust stains. Add in scuff marks from maintenance crews, paint faded from the sun or chipped paint, and you can see that aircraft "weather" rapidly.

Armor gets dirty quickly. Just a single off-road operation will make a tank or soft-skinned vehicle filthy. A moving tank flings earth and dust everywhere, and a lot of it lands on the tank itself. Road wheels gather mud, track

Fig. 1. Before applying the dark wash, bathe the entire model with a soft brush and clean thinner.

Fig. 2. While the surface is still damp, apply the wash over the entire model with a soft, wide, flat brush.

Fig. 3. Wipe the paint out of the brush on a clean cloth.

Fig. 4. Dry-brushing makes the high points stand out. With little pigment left on the brush, lightly wipe raised details.

Fig. 5. Rubbing pastel chalks on sandpaper yields little piles of pastel dust.

rusts, and gears wear; soon, a tank looks pretty grungy.

Rust — the seemingly inevitable oxidation of iron — is a common sight on tank tracks, ships, and equipment.

As you can see, weathering is an important element in the creation of a realistic model.

There are many ways to weather models with many fascinating techniques. Let's go over the three most commonly used methods of weathering: washes, dry-brushing, and pastels. None of these is particularly difficult — in fact, weathering with these techniques is fun!

Washes. In modeling, a "wash" is not a cleaning method, but a weathering technique. A wash adds depth to the appearance of a model by accentuating shadows in corners and crevices. Washes are usually accomplished with a drastically thinned dark paint — "dirty thinner" is closer to the truth. A wash deposits dark color in recessed panel lines and hinge lines that normally would accumulate grease and grime.

You don't want to overdo the wash. Start with the base color of the model darkened with black or dark gray. Thin this color extensively with mineral spirits for enamels, or use water or an alcohol/water mix for water-base paints. *Never* use lacquer-based paint or thinner for washes.

Before you apply the wash, brush clean thinner over the model, Fig. 1. This step prepares the surface and improves the flow of the wash. Now apply the wash with a soft, wide, flat brush, Fig. 2. As the thinner dries, the dark pigment will settle into the low spots.

Dry-brushing. Just as "washing" deepens shadows, dry-brushing emphasizes high points. The idea behind dry-brushing is to lighten the points of a model that protrude from the surface: rivets, wheel hubs, outside corners, hinges, and so forth. These areas would naturally wear faster and catch more light, and we're trying to duplicate those effects with paint.

Dry-brushing starts with the base color, only this time we'll lighten it with white. Use a flat brush again and pick up some of the lightened paint. Now rub the brush on a clean rag or paper until almost all the paint comes off, Fig. 3. Notice that although the paint is nearly gone from the brush, the hairs are colored by the paint. Lightly brush the model's surface, Fig. 4. The pigment rubs off on high points and accentuates

51

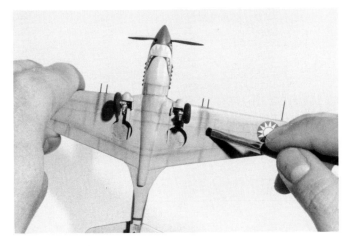

Fig. 7. Pastels applied with a stubble brush are perfect for exhaust and smoke stains.

Fig. 8. A cotton swab will feather pastel weathering. If you rub off too much, simply reapply your pastels.

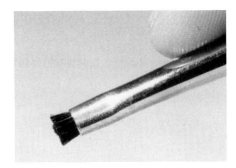

Fig. 6. A stubble brush is made by cutting down an old paintbrush.

them. If you see paint streaks, the brush is too wet; if you don't see any color, the brush is too dry. After the first overall dry-brushing, lighten the base color even more with white. Now dry-brush the highest points again.

Dry-brushing takes practice, so experiment on an old model first. Expect that the brush will wear out, too. If you lighten too much, try dry-brushing with the base color to tone down the highlights. The amount of dry-brushing is a matter of taste; be subtle as you weather your model.

Pastels. My favorite weathering technique is applying pastels. Artists' pastel chalks come in a variety of colors; for model weathering you'll be using white, light gray, medium gray, yellow ochre, raw sienna, burnt sienna, raw umber, burnt umber, and black. Siennas are reddish browns, good for simulating rust and rust stains. Umbers are dark browns, good for simulating dirt, smoke, and grease stains.

Rub each pastel color on sandpaper to produce a tiny pile of pastel dust, Fig. 5. Don't apply the chalk stick directly to the model. I use three alternatives to apply the pastel dust: a soft flat brush, cotton swabs, and a stubble brush I made by cutting down an old paintbrush, Fig. 6.

Use a mixture of burnt sienna, me-

Fig. 9. A light application of light or medium gray pastel will effectively represent dust. Simply blow the excess pastel dust off the model.

dium gray, and a touch of black pastel dust for exhaust stains on aircraft. Pound the stubble brush into the pile of mixed dust, then drag it along the model surface in the direction the exhaust would naturally take across the aircraft, Fig. 7. Let up on the pressure as you move to the rear to simulate the diffusion of the exhaust. Rub a cotton swab over the area to feather the stains even more, Fig. 8.

For general dusting, apply light or medium gray over the entire model with a soft brush, Fig. 9. A light application will soften the appearance of the model. Blow the excess dust off. Since pastel chalk dust doesn't bond to the paint, fingerprints will show if you handle the model. You can apply a clear coat over the pastels, but you may find that it will tone down the final color of the model. You can counteract

this effect by applying more pastels than necessary. This is especially true with light pastels over dark colors, but it is not so evident with dark pastels on light colors.

Where to weather. The degree of weathering is up to you. You can make your model appear factory-fresh, badly deteriorated, or somewhere in between. Whatever you choose, you will want to apply weathering to the correct areas of the model. Here's a short list of target areas for weathering:

Aircraft. Grease smears from hinge lines; oil leaks around engine cowlings; powder stains from gun blast; smoke stains from exhaust stacks; hydraulic fluid from landing gear struts; dirt from wheels around wheel wells; worn panel lines from maintenance; scuff marks on crew-boarding paths; fuel stains around filler caps.

Fig. 11. Sanding the bottoms of model aircraft tires improves their appearance. Note the gray-painted tread area, too.

Fig. 10. Sanding treads makes model tires look less glossy than the sidewalls.

Armor. Powder stains on gun barrel tips; rust on track; mud accumulated around wheels; worn drive wheel sprockets and guide teeth; fuel stains around filler caps; smoke stains on exhaust; grease from wheel hubs; scuff marks around access hatches; and dust everywhere.

Ships. Smoke stains on exhaust pipe caps; rust from bilge pipes and on some panel lines; salt stains lightening forward panels; faded wood decks; grease on cables and bearing surfaces; and powder burns around gun barrel tips.

Autos. Worn tire tread, upholstery, and convertible tops; rusty tail pipes; dirt on engine underneath hood. There aren't many weathering possibilities for autos unless you model a dirt racer (in that case, mud splatters all over, especially around wheels; smoke stains on exhaust tips.)

A word or two about tires. To make model car tires look more realistic, sand the tread area with 400-grit sandpaper and brush off the dust, Fig. 10.

Now the tread looks lighter and less glossy than the sidewalls.

The same goes for aircraft tires. Here, instead of sanding, you'll want to simulate the worn tread area with dark gray paint. Another trick with aircraft tires is to sand the bottoms flat, Fig. 11. This step makes the model rest more realistically on a base or shelf and reduces its toylike appearance.

Weathering is your final chance to make your model look realistic. But keep in mind that bad or inappropriate weathering can ruin the appearance of your model. Subtlety is your watchword. And, of course, practice.

We'll wrap up FSM's Finishing School next chapter when we discuss modeling disasters and their solutions. Oh, by the way, we'll have a little quiz, too!

HOMEWORK ASSIGNMENT 11
BASIC WEATHERING

Materials: Painted model, base color paint, thinner, soft flat brushes, black paint, white paint, cotton swabs, clean cloth, sandpaper, pastel chalks.

☐ Reread this lesson.
☐ Determine what parts of the model should be weathered.
☐ Make a wash by mixing the base color, a little black paint, and a lot of thinner.
☐ Bathe the model with clean thinner.
☐ Brush on the wash, letting it flow into low spots and corners.
☐ Let the model dry thoroughly.
☐ Mix the base color with white paint.
☐ After dipping the brush into the lightened base color, rub the paint out on a clean cloth.
☐ Lightly wipe the brush on the model's high points.
☐ Mix the lightened base color with more white and repeat the dry-brushing process.
☐ Rub pastel chalks on sandpaper to make little piles of pastel dust.
☐ Apply pastel dust with a soft brush or a stubble brush.
☐ Feather pastels with a cotton swab.

LESSON 12:
Dealing with disasters

What can go wrong might go wrong

BY PAUL BOYER

WELL, LIKE ALL students attending the last class of the session, you guys are probably ready to get out of here and start applying everything you've learned. But the road to modeling success is strewn with bumps and potholes, and it's likely you'll hit one at the worst possible moment.

Don't look so crushed. I've told you that FSM's Finishing School alone isn't enough to help you learn to finish models better. Practice is the key. I've found that the more models I build, the fewer problems I encounter. You, too, will learn to anticipate pitfalls and work around them. With experience, you'll know that picking up a freshly painted model will leave fingerprints in the paint, that using incompatible coats of paints can ruin the finish, that decals can tangle and tear, and so forth.

Let's go over major roadblocks in the way to a beautifully finished model. Later, we'll take the final exam. What? Come, now! You didn't expect to complete the course without a test, did you?

Cracked paint. This is one disaster with no easy solution. Paint cracks when coats of paint shrink at different rates as they cure, Fig. 1. Gloss acrylic

paints seem especially prone to this condition. It can be caused by incompatible paints and thinners, poor paint adhesion, or a paint formula that doesn't allow the paint to flex.

Since cracking doesn't usually show up until a few days or even weeks after you've completed the model, you'll have to strip the paint and decals and start finishing the model again.

Stripping paint from a model is a messy task. Use Polly S ELO (Easy Lift

Off) for your first attempt. If that doesn't work, spray a commercial oven cleaner on the model or immerse it in hydraulic brake fluid. (Make sure you handle these substances with chemical-resistant gloves.) After the chemicals soften the paint, wash the model with soap and water and dry it thoroughly before repainting.

Jack Frost nipping at your model. Your model is painted and decaled, and you're all set to apply the clear flat

Fig. 1. Cracked paint has no easy solution. You'll have to strip the paint and reapply.

Fig. 2. Clear flat may turn frosty if it has been insufficiently stirred or improperly thinned.

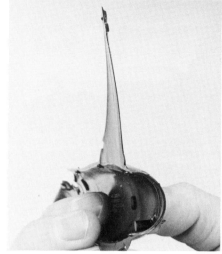

Fig. 3. Warming a warped plastic part in hot water and bending against the warp is an easy fix.

coat. Everything is going smoothly, but you notice the clear flat dries frosty white, Fig. 2. What's happening here? How can you fix this?

There are three probable causes for this condition. The least likely is excess humidity. In a humid environment, water vapor can attach itself to spray-paint particles, land on the model, and become trapped. Professional painters call this condition "blushing."

Another cause is paint formula incompatibility. Some clear coats dissolve the paint on your model, creating a condition called "crazing." This often looks like frost.

The most likely cause of frosting is that you didn't stir or thin the clear flat coat enough. Too much flattening agent (tiny bits of talc or wax) in relation to vehicle (the binder) results. Clear flat coats should be thinned with at least an equal amount of the thinner made for the paint.

The only way to fix this condition is to strip the clear flat from the model as soon as possible. The longer you wait,

the more difficulty you'll have removing the frosted clear coat. Try denatured alcohol first. It can remove many uncured clear coats with only minor risk to the underlying color. However, it may also destroy the decals. (The only answer to that is to buy another set of decals and reapply them.)

If denatured alcohol won't remove the clear coat, you will have to use thinner. Thinner, however, can remove the decals *and* the color coats. Be prepared to refinish the entire model.

Twisted kit, sir. Warped parts in injection-molded kits are rare, Fig. 3. Sometimes plastic sprues are still warm exiting the injection-molding machine. If they come to rest twisted, the twist sets as the plastic cools.

The simplest solution to warpage is to heat the parts enough so you can work them back to their proper shape. Now don't go running for a torch: You can reset most warped parts with hot water and careful bending. First heat a pot of water large enough to immerse the warped part. You don't want the

water boiling, but it should be uncomfortable for your finger. Dip the part into the water for 30 seconds or so, heating the plastic so you can bend it without breaking it. Make sure that the part doesn't touch the bottom or the side of the pot — the metal could be hot enough to melt the plastic and ruin the part.

Take the part out of the hot water and immediately bend it opposite the warp and beyond the final correct position. Bend a little bit at a time and hold it for another 30 seconds or so. As the plastic cools, the bend you are applying will set, counteracting the warp.

You can fix minor warping without such kitchen wizardry. To attach a warped part to an unwarped larger part, glue the part a little at a time and clamp it as you go, Fig. 4. After the cement has set, glue and clamp a little farther along; repeat until the parts are completely cemented.

Disintegrating decals. This one traps many unsuspecting modelers. Let's say Gerry over here has assembled all the necessary tools and materials for a session of decaling. He dips the first one in water; as he gently slides the decal onto the model, it shatters in a zillion pieces, Fig. 5. No! This isn't supposed to happen!

Decal disintegration usually stems from a clear carrier film that is too thin, but old decals may crack, too. Unfortunately, you can't tell ahead of time if a decal has this problem — you have to try it first. Pick a marking you don't need on the model. Choose one with a lot of clear carrier between image areas, such as a string of letters or numbers. If the decal comes off the backing paper in one piece, the other decals on the sheet should be okay.

If the decal disintegrates, apply a new clear carrier film over the rest of

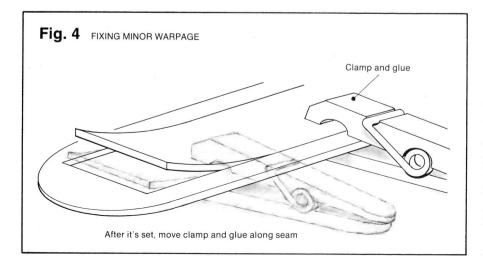

Fig. 4 FIXING MINOR WARPAGE

Clamp and glue

After it's set, move clamp and glue along seam

Fig. 5. Decals can shatter if the clear carrier film isn't strong enough to hold the image together.

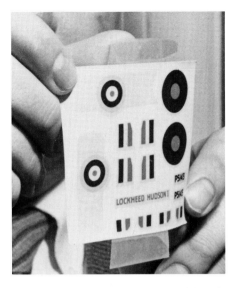

Fig. 6. An easy solution to yellowed decals is to tape them to a window and let the sun bleach out the yellow.

the sheet. Airbrush a coat of clear gloss or clear flat over the entire decal sheet. It's better to use enamel or lacquer here; acrylics not completely cured will dissolve in water.

Now you have a decal with an overall clear carrier film. That means you'll need to cut around each image to separate it from the rest. Usually, setting solutions will still work on these modified decals.

Ol' yeller decals. How many of you have pulled the decals from an old kit and found the clear carrier film yellowed with age? Yeah, just about all of you. Well, you might prefer aftermarket decals, but these oldies can still be used. The yellow comes from a chemical reaction of the clear carrier and the backing paper. Over time, this causes the carrier to yellow.

You could simply bleach the yellow out with sunlight. Tape the decal to the inside surface of a sunny window, Fig. 6. Make sure that this window doesn't "sweat" — humidity inside your house condenses on cool windows. This moisture can trigger the water-activated adhesive and ruin the decals. Leave the decal in the window for a few weeks; check it periodically. The sunlight will bleach out the yellow before it begins to fade the colors of the decals.

Use the decals as soon as you can. If you put the decals away, the chemical process will again turn the clear carrier yellow.

Glue on clear plastic. Perhaps everyone has had this accident at one time or another. You get plastic cement on a clear part. The part appears ruined; replacing it with a part from another kit will be expensive. Don't despair. First let the cement dry thoroughly: Anything you do to soft plastic will only make the problem worse.

Starting with 400-grit wet-or-dry sandpaper, wet sand the offending area with a circular motion. Yes, this looks awful, doesn't it? Now the part is all scratched and worse-looking than before! Now switch to wet 600-grit paper and sand the area again. The 600-grit paper will smooth out the scratches

---

FSM'S FINISHING SCHOOL
FINAL EXAM

The final examination is multiple choice. You have all the time in the world to complete the exam. Feel free to look back over past lessons for the answers. Begin.

1. What happens if you use too much glue? (Lesson 1: Glues, fillers, and eliminating seams)
A. The parts stick too well
B. The glue dries too fast
C. The parts melt and distort
D. Nothing happens

2. What is the advantage of using gap-filling super glue and an accelerator to fill seams and depressions? (Lesson 1)
A. It sets quickly
B. You can sand seams right away
C. It bonds to the model well
D. All of the above

3. Why should a model be washed before painting? (Lesson 2: Preparing to paint)
A. It prevents the spread of germs
B. It removes oils, release agents, and fingerprints that might affect paint adhesion
C. It removes excess glue and filler
D. All of the above

4. Why use a primer? (Lesson 2)
A. You can see surface imperfections more easily

B. It improves the adhesion of the color coats
C. Both A and B
D. It kills time

5. Why shouldn't you store thinned paint? (Lesson 3: Modeling paints)
A. The thinner might eat through the bottle
B. Adding thinner could upset the paint formula and after a few days, it could become unusable
C. Thinner makes the color turn black after a few days
D. There's no reason not to store thinned paint

6. Find the true statement about acrylic modeling paints: (Lesson 3)
A. They are nontoxic
B. They are water soluble
C. They adhere better than enamels or lacquers
D. All of the above are true

7. What does a wetting agent do to Polly S acrylic paint? (Lesson 4: Brush painting)
A. It thins the paint
B. It thickens the paint
C. It makes the paint stick better
D. It allows the paint to flow better

8. How should paint be brushed on a model? (Lesson 4)
A. Dabbing it on
B. Using long strokes until the brush runs out of paint
C. Using short, quick strokes
D. Using your finger

9. Why warm a spray can before painting? (Lesson 5: Painting with spray cans)
A. Exploding a spray can is the quickest way to paint
B. Warm paint sprays better and settles smoothly
C. Immersing the spray can in warm water makes the paint dry quicker
D. Warming the can releases the label

10. What's the best way to get a glossy finish from spray paint? (Lesson 5)
A. Spray the model nonstop until all the paint is gone
B. Wait at least a month between coats
C. Hold the can about one inch away from the model
D. Dust on the first coat, spray the second coat a little heavier, and apply a wet third coat

11. Is a spray booth a good investment? (Lesson 6: Safety with glues, paints, and thinners)
A. Yes, because many modeling materials contain toxic chemicals
B. Yes, because it helps the economy
C. No, because modeling is a safe hobby
D. No, because I paint in a big room

12. True or false: Super glue releases cyanide gas. (Lesson 6)

from the 400-grit paper. Next use 1,000- or 1,200-grit paper (look for it at automotive-supply stores), and repeat the process. Keep using that circular motion. You'll see that the clear plastic is looking better and better.

Now apply automotive polishing compound, plastic polish, or even toothpaste to the area with a clean cloth, Fig. 7. Polish and buff with the cloth. A final coat of Future acrylic floor finish, and the clear part looks as good as new.

Fingerprints. The adage "haste makes waste" was obviously coined by a modeler. You can't wait to pick up the model you painted a few hours ago. When you set it down again, you see them — great big fingerprints in the paint, Fig. 8. AAARGH! Now that you've learned your lesson, don't touch the model until the paint is cured: Wait a day for most flat paints, a couple of days for gloss paints.

Now, just as you did with the glue marks on clear plastic, use wet 600-grit paper and lightly sand the blemished area. Rinse off sanding dust, then go to work with polishing compound, plastic polish, or toothpaste.

Orange peel gloss. Even after carefully applying gloss paint, the finish isn't really smooth. It seems shiny, but has a soft, lumpy appearance. This is "orange peel," usually caused by not mixing enough thinner into the paint before airbrushing.

To fix orange peel, wait until the paint is completely cured — a few days, a week to be on the safe side. Lightly sand the finish with wet 600-grit paper, then polish as outlined above. Sometimes you'll polish the paint off the high spots. You'll then have to spray on another coat of paint and repeat the process if necessary.

Graduation. I'm not going to bore you with a long-winded commencement speech. I hope that this course

Fig. 7. Spilled glue on a clear part isn't the end of the world. Sanding and polishing will restore the clarity.

Fig. 8. Ooooh noooo, Mister Hand! What have you done? Handling fresh paint is an easily preventable disaster.

has helped you avoid finishing problems and that it helps you create more beautiful models. Please remember that it's not enough for you to know how to do it. You have to practice. The more models you build, the better each one will look. Good luck, my friends! **FSM**

HOMEWORK ASSIGNMENT 12

DEALING WITH DISASTERS

☐ Reread this lesson.
☐ Keep your wits about you!
☐ Practice, practice, practice.

---

13. Why should you thin paint for airbrushing? (Lesson 7: Basic airbrushing)
  A. It's more economical
  B. Thinned paint flows through the nozzle better
  C. Thinned paint dries quicker
  D. Thinning paint doesn't help at all

14. How often should you clean your airbrush? (Lesson 7)
  A. An airbrush cleans itself
  B. Once a year
  C. After every painting session
  D. Only after using black paint

15. When airbrushing a multicolor camouflage scheme, which color should you start with? (Lesson 8: Advanced airbrushing)
  A. The lightest color
  B. The darkest color
  C. Any color is okay
  D. Fluorescent red

16. When should you remove masking tape? (Lesson 8)
  A. Before the paint is dry
  B. As soon as the paint is dry to the touch
  C. After one day
  D. After one week

17. Why do you need a smooth surface for natural metal finishes? (Lesson 9: Natural metal finishes)
  A. Paints stick better
  B. You don't need a smooth surface

  C. Buffing a rough surface will wear out the cloth
  D. Natural metal finishes show every scratch, pit, and ripple

18. Bare-Metal Foil is handy for: (Lesson 9)
  A. Wrapping sandwiches
  B. Covering surface imperfections
  C. Chrome trim on auto and truck models
  D. All of the above

19. How can you prevent a decal from "silvering"? (Lesson 10: Applying decals)
  A. Use gloss paints or a clear gloss underneath the decals
  B. Use flat paints or a clear flat underneath the decals
  C. Never use silver paint
  D. Apply a drop of liquid cement to the decal

20. A decal solvent will: (Lesson 10)
  A. Remove decals
  B. Dissolve decals until they vanish
  C. Ruin paint
  D. Soften decals and allow them to conform to the model's surface

21. Weathering a model will: (Lesson 11: Basic weathering)
  A. Make it look more realistic
  B. Prevent weather from damaging the finish
  C. Ruin the finish
  D. Have little or no effect on the model

22. A "wash" will: (Lesson 11)
  A. Clean the model
  B. Keep the oil from your fingers off the model
  C. Add depth and accentuate shadows
  D. Brighten high points

23. What's the best way to fix a warped plastic part? (Lesson 12: Dealing with disasters)
  A. Break the warped section off and glue it back on straight
  B. Heat it in an oven for one hour at 450 degrees
  C. Pop it in the freezer for one hour
  D. Immerse it in hot water and bend the part carefully

24. How can you repair clear parts blemished by glue? (Lesson 12)
  A. The part is ruined; just buy a new one
  B. Hold the clear part over a flame until the blemish disappears
  C. Tape it in a window and let sunlight bleach it out
  D. Use wet sandpaper and polish to remove the blemish

ANSWERS

1. C	7. D	13. B	19. A
2. D	8. C	14. C	20. D
3. B	9. B	15. A	21. A
4. C	10. D	16. B	22. C
5. B	11. A	17. D	23. D
6. B	12. False	18. C	24. D

Acrylic paints may change our thoughts about painting models. Here Paul applies Gunze Sangyo Aqueous Hobby Color Extra Dark Sea Grey to a Fujimi FG. 1 Phantom.

Using acrylic modeling paints

These revolutionary paints may change our hobby

BY PAUL BOYER

REVOLUTIONARY? Paint is paint, right? Wrong. Some of the ever-present dangers of our hobby are potentially hazardous chemicals: Glues, paints, and thinners can be harmful — even fatal — if misused. Even occasional use of some paints and glues can be harmful when the overspray and fumes rising from open paint and thinner containers are inhaled.

I confess that I've been a Floquil paint fan since I first tried it in 1971. Floquil's solvent, Dio-Sol, contains xylene, which etches the surface of plastic ever so slightly if properly airbrushed. It also has a strong odor. I used to mix my own Federal Standard 595 matches

with the standard Floquil railroad colors. I've also used enamels: Testor Model Master, Pactra, Humbrol, and others. I don't know what years of exposure to the fumes from these paints and thinners have done to me, but I recommend that you ventilate your work area properly and use a respirator or a filtering device over your nose and mouth.

For years we've heard cautions about the fumes from glue and paint, and, heeding those warnings, cautious modelers have quietly (and safely) used acrylic paints.

They're nontoxic. Nontoxic doesn't necessarily mean that something is completely safe to use. If you swallow enough acrylic paint, you'll probably get sick. But in regular use, acrylics of-

fer safety features that no enamel or lacquer can match. Depending on what you use for thinner, acrylic fumes aren't dangerous. Most acrylics have little odor and their thinners — water and alcohol — won't poison your air.

Nontoxic doesn't mean nonflammable. Although I didn't test for it, some acrylics thinned with alcohol compounds can ignite, but they certainly present less hazard than conventional paints and thinners.

To prepare this article I tested five brands of acrylic paint, Fig. 1. Let's take a brief look at each product line.

● **Badger Air-Opaque.** These paints are mostly standard colors (red, blue, yellow) produced specifically for airbrushing. Weathering sets for railroad models and scenery fill out this 43-

Fig. 1 ACRYLIC MODELING PAINTS

Brand and Manufacturer	No. of Colors	Cost per ml	Hand brush	Airbrush	Recommended thinner and paint:thin ratio	Strengths	Weaknesses
Badger Air-Opaque Badger Airbrush Co. 9128 W. Belmont Franklin Park, IL 60131	43	8.4¢	F	G	2:1 alcohol or water/alcohol	Plastic squeeze bottle, economical	Poor adhesion limited color range, hard to find
Gunze Sangyo Aqueous Hobby Color Distributed by Marco Polo Import Inc. 2239 Tyler Ave., Unit A South El Monte, CA 91733	146	13.9¢	G	VG	2:1 alcohol or water/alcohol	Wide color range, spill-resistant bottles, good finish, good adhesion, good color accuracy	Most expensive, hard to find
Pactra Acrylic Paint Pactra Coatings, Inc. 420 S. 11th Ave. Upland, CA 91786	48	9.0¢	VG	VG	2:1 alcohol or water/alcohol	Excellent color accuracy, good adhesion, economical	Limited color range, hard to find
Polly S Floquil-Polly S Color Corp. Route 30 North Amsterdam, NY 12010-9204	174	7.9¢	E	F	1:1 alcohol or water/alcohol	Widest color range, easy to find, least expensive, best hand brushed, good adhesion	Questionable color accuracy, difficult to airbrush
Tamiya Color Acrylic Paint Distributed by Model Rectifier Corp. 2500 Woodbridge Ave. Edison, NJ 08817	70	8.6¢	G	VG	2:1 alcohol or alcohol/water	Easy to find, spill-resistant bottles, economical, good adhesion	Limited color range

F = Fair
G = Good
VG = Very Good
E = Excellent

color line. Air-Opaque sprays well when thinned with water, alcohol, or a mix of the two, but it's too thin for hand brushing. Unique among hobby paints is the 1-ounce (30 ml) plastic squeeze bottle. Each costs $2.50.

• **Gunze Sangyo Aqueous Hobby Color.** If you've built recent Hasegawa, Fujimi, or Gunze Sangyo kits, you may have wondered what the color number recommendations in the instructions refer to. They call for Gunze Sangyo Aqueous Hobby Colors from Japan. Gunze paint is thin and has little odor. It can be airbrushed from the bottle, but it is better thinned. Hand brushing is difficult because multiple coats are needed. The color range is extensive (146) and features standard colors, U. S. FS 595 colors, current Israeli and British shades, World War Two camouflage colors, clear tints, and metallics. It can be thinned with water, alcohol, or an alcohol/water mix. Gunze Sangyo also makes Mr. Color, an acrylic lacquer line, but these are not nontoxic. Aqueous Hobby Colors come in 10 ml bottles for $1.39. A few colors are available in spray cans.

• **Pactra Acrylic Paints.** Introduced recently, Pactra Acrylic is also thin, with a slight odor. The 48-color line includes standard colors, Vietnamera FS 595 colors, and WWII camouflage shades. It can be thinned with

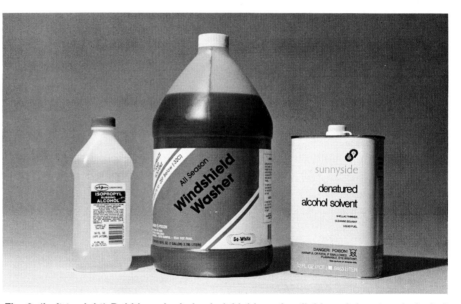

Fig. 2. (Left to right) Rubbing alcohol, windshield washer fluid, and denatured alcohol can be used to thin acrylic paints. Although the fumes from these liquids aren't dangerous, ingesting them can be harmful or fatal — use them with caution.

water, alcohol, or a mix. It is a little thicker than Gunze and better for hand brushing. Each two-thirds-ounce (20ml) bottle sells for $1.79.

• **Polly S.** The first acrylic modeling paint was Polly S, introduced in 1970. I've used Polly S for many years — it's thick and perfect for hand brushing (see section on page 16). Airbrushing is

difficult, but can be done. Polly S has the widest range of colors of all the modeling acrylics (174, although some are duplicated), including standard colors, U. S. FS 595 colors, WWII camouflage colors, and a line of fantasy colors. There is also a 24-color line of railroad paints. Polly S has little odor and thins with water, alcohol, or a mix

Fig. 3. Paul tested each acrylic on a sheet of white styrene. After a little practice, you can spray a fine line with acrylic paint thinned with alcohol.

of the two. It comes in ½-ounce (15 ml) bottles for $1.19.

● **Tamiya Color.** Tamiya paints from Japan were the first thin acrylics, airbrushable right out of the bottle (but better when thinned). Tamiya goes on okay with a brush, but not as well as Polly S. The odor is the most noticeable of all the acrylics — some find it offensive, but the fumes are still nontoxic. The paint can be thinned with Tamiya's thinner, alcohol, water, or an alcohol/water mix. Tamiya's range (70) includes standard colors, generic military shades, clear tints, and metallics. Tamiya also has an enamel line and polycarbonate paints for Lexan radio-control car bodies. Tamiya's 23 ml bottles sell for $1.98.

Color accuracy. Three of the five acrylic paint lines (Gunze Sangyo, Pactra, and Polly S) claimed to match specific color references such as FS 595, the color chip standards for paints used by the government for camouflage on aircraft, armor, and other equipment. I picked four commonly used FS colors and hand brushed a swatch of each brand on white styrene, let it dry, and compared it to the FS 595 color chips. The colors I tested were Olive Drab (FS 34087), SEA camouflage Olive Green (FS 34102), Light Gull Gray (FS 36440), and Light Compass Ghost Gray (FS 36375).

Real Olive Drab is notorious for color shift, fading and weathering soon after application, but there is a standard color chip. (Incidentally, the latest issue of FS 595 doesn't have this color, so I had to refer to an old issue.) Compared to it, Gunze Sangyo Olive Drab H304 is a little too brown, Pactra A30 is a perfect match, and Polly S 500832 is too gray. (Although Tamiya's paints don't claim to match any color standard, I checked its Olive Drab XF-62 —

it's too dark and too green.) For SEA Olive Green, Gunze Sangyo H303 is just a tad too green, Pactra A33 is again a perfect match, and Polly S 500834 is considerably greener. Light Gull Gray from Gunze (H315, actually glossy FS 16440) is a perfect match as is Pactra A43, while Polly S 500825 is too dark. Light Compass Ghost Gray from Gunze (H308) is a little on the purple side, Pactra A42 is a perfect match, and Polly S 500836 is a little yellow.

Although this is certainly not an exhaustive comparison, it appears that Pactra has done the best job in matching FS 595 colors. If you're a color fanatic, this may be important, but many modelers will simply buy the color they need, paint the model, and be happy with the results. A word of caution: Don't judge the color of paint by looking at it in the bottle or while it is still wet. All the Pactra paints looked much too light until they dried.

Cheap thinner. Since all the acrylics can be thinned with water, you don't have to spend money on exotic thinners, Fig. 2. However, airbrushing performance improved when the paints were thinned with alcohol or a water/alcohol mixture. Alcohol is actually "wetter" than water; it has less surface tension — that's what causes water to bead up — and acts as a wetting agent, improving the paint's flow.

I tried rubbing alcohol (70 percent isopropyl, about 79 cents per pint at the drugstore), denatured alcohol (about $2.00 per quart at the hardware store), and windshield washer fluid (a water/alcohol/detergent mix, about $1.00 per gallon at gas stations); all worked about the same and better than straight water.

Windshield washer fluid concerned me because it contains a coloring agent

(blue or pink). I thought this might shift the color of the paint, so I mixed one part with two parts Gunze Sangyo flat white and compared it with paint thinned with rubbing alcohol. The difference is barely perceptible and, since white tends to yellow with age, the extra blue would help counter it. I found no color shift when testing the light gray paints thinned with windshield washer fluid.

Testing. If you've spent months adjusting paint and thinner ratios, raising and lowering air pressure, and trying other tricks to master the art of airbrushing your favorite paint, you may not welcome a switch to something new. After all, if you've finally got it all figured out, why should you start over? How do acrylics spray through an airbrush? Do they stick to plastic? Will decal solvents affect acrylic paints? And finally, does the safety issue warrant switching to acrylics? That's a big question, so I set out to test the paints to answer several more-manageable ones.

For the tests, I used a Badger 350 single-action airbrush with an air pressure of 30 psi. I chose a light gray color from each line and airbrushed it onto clean white sheet styrene, Fig. 3. I thinned one part Polly S with one part thinner, but I thinned the other colors two parts paint to one part thinner. Each brand was also sprayed without thinning to see how it performed right out of the bottle.

I also experimented with different thinners: straight water, straight denatured alcohol, straight isopropyl alcohol, and straight windshield washer, then cut each alcohol with equal amounts of water. I also tried Tamiya Thinner with Tamiya acrylics. The people at Marco Polo Import suggested using Mr. Thinner (thinner for acrylic lacquer) with the Gunze paints. It works, but it is toxic and negates the biggest benefit of the nontoxic paint.

Thinning with water worked with all the brands I tested. It's the safest thinner but it's also the most difficult to use. Water produced the smoothest coats of paint, but they were less opaque — it took more coats to produce satisfactory coverage.

Thinning with straight alcohol or a 50:50 mix of alcohol and water made the paint flow better. There was no detectable difference between types of alcohol or between straight and diluted alcohol. I checked for texture, coverage, nozzle clogs, and minimum spray pattern with each paint/thinner mixture. The drying time of acrylics thinned with water was longer than acrylics thinned with alcohol, but neither was appreciably longer than enamels. After the paint dried, I tested for adhesion by flexing the sheet styrene

Fig. 4. Badger Air-Opaque didn't stick to styrene regardless of the thinner used.

to see if the paint would chip off.

Straight from the bottle, Badger had the second roughest texture. When thinned with water it was less opaque but sprayed better; alcohol makes it spread more evenly. Badger flunked the adhesion test, though — it cracked when I bent the styrene and flaked away with a touch of my finger, Fig. 4. Badger Air-Opaque may work fine on absorbent materials, but they don't stick well to plastic.

Gunze Sangyo sprayed well from the bottle, but it dried a little pebbly. It's better when thinned with alcohol or an alcohol/water mix, and I was able to spray a fine line without clogging the airbrush tip. When dry, Gunze has a semi-gloss sheen unique among the acrylics, and that may help decal application. Gunze also did well in the adhesion test; there was no cracking and flaking off the flexed plastic.

Pactra's performance was similar to Gunze's — slightly rough straight out of the bottle, smoother when thinned. Again, I was able to maintain a fine line with the airbrush. Pactra adhered well to styrene.

Polly S did not spray well out of the bottle — it's just too thick. It was difficult to spray a fine line and the paint went on and dried lumpy on the styrene. Polly S's performance improved when thinned with water, although it wasn't smooth. When thinned with alcohol, it sprayed much better and a little smoother, but Polly S still had the roughest texture of all. I had occasional clogs when I painted a fine line with the airbrush. Polly S adhered well.

Tamiya sprayed well right out of the bottle, but improved slightly when thinned. I found no appreciable advantage of Tamiya's thinner over alcohol when thinning Tamiya paints. I was able to obtain a fine line with the airbrush without clogging the tip, and Tamiya acrylics adhered well to styrene.

Glossy acrylics. With the exception of Badger, all the acrylic lines feature glossy paints. I picked a dark blue gloss from each brand, diluted each with an alcohol water mixture (Polly S 1:1, the others 2:1), and airbrushed them onto white sheet styrene. All the brands sprayed easily, resulting in a slightly rippled gloss. Of the four, Polly S had the poorest gloss; the others were better and about equal in sheen.

Cleanup. One of the beauties of acrylic paint is that you don't need powerful (and poisonous) solvents to clean your brushes, airbrush, and hands — if you clean right away. When wet, acrylics can be removed easily with soap and water, but when dry, water won't affect them. It's a good idea to keep a small bottle of detergent water handy when airbrushing. After completing a color, *immediately* dip the siphon tube into the soapy water and spray it through the airbrush for a minute or so. This will clear the paint out of the system, and you're ready for the next color.

However, if you let the paint dry in the airbrush, you'll have to carefully disassemble the tip and bathe the parts in lacquer thinner (remember, we were trying to stay away from that stuff). I scrub my airbrush with cotton swabs and pipe cleaners, being careful not to damage the fragile tip.

Decal solvents. Acrylic paints contain water and alcohol, so I suspected that decal solvents (many of which contain water and alcohol) could harm them. To test, I placed drops of plain water, Gunze Sangyo Mr. Mark Softer, Micro Sol, and Micro Set on a piece of styrene painted the day before with glossy blue from Gunze, Pactra, Polly S, and Tamiya. I waited for the drops to evaporate to see if the solvents lifted or stained the paints.

Gunze Sangyo Aqueous Hobby Color was most affected by, strangely, Gunze Mr. Mark Softer, which faded the blue paint. Micro Sol and Micro Set left rings, but did not affect the color. None of the solvents seemed to affect Pactra or Polly S. Mr. Mark Softer made the Tamiya blue fade slightly, but the other solvents had little effect.

Conclusions. If you're used to airbrushing enamels, your first experience spraying acrylics may be upsetting. The first coat of acrylics may come out a little blotchy and appear lumpy, but the following thin coats smooth things out considerably. By adjusting your thinning ratio and air pressure, you'll be able to spray fine lines with little clogging.

Since water's surface tension plays a major role in how acrylics lie down on the model, be sure to wash the model with detergent and water before painting. Oil from your fingers and mold-release agent can repel the water-base paint.

Once you get used to the different techniques needed to apply acrylics, you'll find that they are just as good as standard model enamels. However, the small range of useful colors, lack of gloss paints, and poor adhesion of Badger Air-Opaque colors present problems for modelers.

Gunze Sangyo Aqueous Hobby Color is excellent paint — the range of useful colors is wide, color accuracy is good, and the smooth, semi-gloss sheen gives a good scale effect. But Gunze is the most expensive of the acrylics and has seen limited distribution in this country.

Pactra is certainly one of the best acrylics. Its color accuracy is excellent, with good adhesion, but the choice of colors is limited and the paint is hard to find in hobby stores.

For ease of hand brushing, nothing (not even enamels) can beat Polly S, but its airbrush performance suffers. It has the broadest range of colors, but their accuracy is questionable. Polly S is the most economical acrylic paint.

Tamiya is also excellent paint, but the choice of colors for military subjects is limited. Its available in many hobby shops and the paint represents good value for the money.

So, are they revolutionary? If you have a large investment in enamels or lacquers and you take the required precautions when using them, don't throw them away. However, since acrylics are safer to use, you should seriously consider replacing your enamels and lacquers with acrylics as you use them up. That's what I'm doing! **FSM**

FSM tested 15 airbrush compressors. Our samples included tiny piston compressors, diaphragm units, and the new "silent" compressors.

Choosing an airbrush compressor

FSM tests 15 compressors, tiny to huge, puny to powerful

BY PAUL BOYER

MANY MODELERS paint their models with an airbrush, a miniature spray gun, and employ various sources of compressed gas to power the tool. Airbrush kits often include a small can of propellant and a hose to connect to the valve on the can. These cans hold a limited amount of propellant (about one half hour's worth) and are economical only if you seldom use your airbrush.

A second source is a compressed air cylinder, purchased or leased from industrial gas supply stores. Although silent, the compressed gas (air or carbon

dioxide) runs out eventually and the cylinder must be recharged. This means hauling it to the nearest dealer, paying for the gas, and hauling it back — and it's a lot heavier when it's full.

The third alternative (and the most popular) is a motor-driven air compressor. There are dozens of air compressors on the market, ranging from tiny piston and small diaphragm compressors (usually found at good hobby stores) to large piston compressors with storage tanks suitable for powering light pneumatic tools and large spray guns. Newcomers to the compressor market are the "silent" or "refrigerator" type. These relatively quiet pis-

Fig. 1. An in-line moisture trap keeps condensed water from reaching the airbrush.

ton units have small storage tanks and large price tags.

Compressor types. All compressors work on the same principle: An electric motor turns an eccentric wheel which causes a piston or diaphragm to travel up and down in a cylinder. As the piston or diaphragm descends, air is drawn into the cylinder through a simple flapper or reed valve. As it ascends, air pressure closes the intake valve and

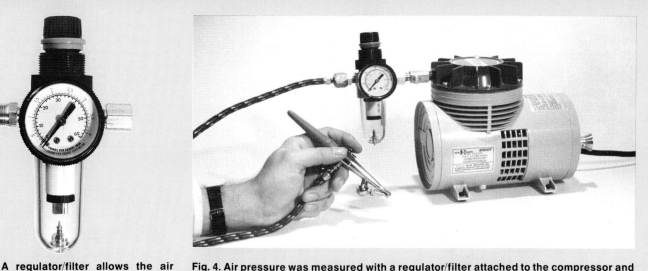

Fig. 2. A regulator/filter allows the air pressure to be adjusted.

Fig. 4. Air pressure was measured with a regulator/filter attached to the compressor and Paasche Model H airbrush connected with a 6′ braided hose.

opens a similar but smaller outlet valve. Since the outlet is smaller than the intake, the exiting air is under pressure as it travels through the hose to the airbrush.

Diaphragm compressors use a flat-headed connecting rod with a flexible disk (diaphragm) mounted on it. Piston compressors use a rigid piston similar to those found in an automobile engine. Most modern diaphragm and piston compressors have sealed bearings and don't require oil.

Small diaphragm and piston compressors are usually inexpensive and can last a long time when properly used. They have limitations — they're noisy and it's difficult to regulate the air pressure they supply. Since many run continuously they get hot, and if you're not careful the heat can warp and bind the moving parts. Some simple compressors have automatic shutoff switches or pressure-bleed valves to prevent meltdowns. Although such compressors run at high speed, the air coming through the air line pulses with each compression stroke.

Some larger compressors have holding tanks — the compressed air fills the tank and, when full, a sensor shuts off the compressor until the air pressure in the tank drops to a set level. Then the motor automatically switches on to refill the tank. This system has three advantages: Since the compressor doesn't have to run continuously, there's less noise; there's less wear and tear on the working parts; and the storage tank provides constant pressure with no pulsations. Storage-tank compressors usually have a regulator to vary the air pressure going to the air line.

Silent compressors are piston units that drive small amounts of air into a storage tank. All silent compressors use light oil to lubricate the working parts. All the units we tested included

a bottle of oil and some were shipped with oil already added. The oil is poured into a small tube until the proper level is viewed in a clear bubble on the side of the unit. Read the instructions carefully and maintain the proper oil level. Operation without oil can ruin an expensive investment.

What to look for. Price is probably the most important factor when you first consider purchasing a compressor. A compressor will probably be your most expensive modeling tool — all of the compressors we tested have list prices over $95.00.

Your wallet may be your first consideration, but don't forget other factors. If you live in an apartment or have

Fig. 3. When your hands are full with airbrush and model, you can turn on the compressor with a foot switch.

family members who sleep while you work on your latest project, you will find noise levels important. Lightweight, easily portable units can allow you to airbrush just about anywhere you have an electrical outlet. You may need to vary the air pressure, so you'll need a regulator. If you have other chores for your compressor, you may need one with increased capacity to power spray guns or pneumatic tools, or to inflate tires, toys, and other equipment.

Compressor accessories. No matter which compressor you choose, invest in an in-line moisture trap, Fig. 1. Whenever air is compressed, it is heated. Air cools as it is released (to the airbrush), causing the water vapor in the air to condense. Water droplets condense in the hose, run to the airbrush, and spurt out with the air and paint mixture. This can be a problem with water-based paints since the droplets will mix easily with the paint, causing thin spots or runs. In-line moisture traps cost around $10.00.

Regulator/filter attachments, Fig. 2, allow you to decrease the output pressure from the compressor, but most small compressors produce the minimum amount you'll need for airbrushing hobby paints. Most compressors with storage tanks include this device or separate regulators and filters. The filter cleans the air of dust and dirt and can remove moisture, but it is not as effective as a moisture trap.

A foot switch is a great idea for compressors without an automatic shut-off feature, Fig. 3. Stepping on the switch turns the compressor on. This eliminates having to reach for the switch (or the cord) when you have your hands full of airbrush and model.

All of these accessories are available from most airbrush dealers.

Testing compressors. FSM obtained 15 sample compressors, ranging from simple piston units, to large ¾-horse-power rigs, to the new "silent" compressors.

We noted the size and weight of each, then measured output air pressures and evaluated relative noise levels. We checked the air output by hooking up a single-action airbrush to a 6′ braided hose. For units without regulators or pressure gauges, we attached a simple regulator/filter to the output fitting, Fig. 4. With the compressor running we noted the pressure on the regulator gauge (static), then depressed the airbrush air button and took the second reading under load.

On the units with storage tanks, we determined how long the units would provide 30 psi through the airbrush before the compressor kicked on, and how long it ran to refill after releasing the air button. We also determined the maximum pressure these units could sustain with the airbrush operating.

SIMPLE COMPRESSORS

Model: No. 80-2 Whirlwind
From: Badger Airbrush Co., 9128 West Belmont Avenue, Franklin Park, Il 60131
Price: $125.00
Type: Oilless piston (1/15 hp)
Size: 8″ long, 4½″ wide, 6″ high
Weight: 5½ lbs.
Air pressure: 17 psi static, 10 psi load
Noise level: Moderate rattle
Features: Pressure relief valve, switch, suction-cup feet, one-year warranty

A tiny oilless piston compressor. The unit works hard, but only produces 10 psi with the airbrush operating — not enough pressure to successfully spray high-viscosity paints. It can spray inks and well-thinned paints. A relief valve prevents air buildup when the airbrush is not operating. Made in Japan.

Model: No. 180-1
From: Badger
Price: $169.00
Type: Oilless diaphragm (1/12 hp)
Size: 8″ long, 5″ wide, 7″ high
Weight: 9 lbs.
Air pressure: 23 psi static, 14 psi load
Noise level: Moderate rattle
Features: Handle, one-year warranty

A typical oilless diaphragm design that is popular among hobbyists. Air pressure of 14 psi is adequate for most hobby paints. The unit operates continuously, but has an internal bleed valve to prevent pressure buildup. As with most diaphragm compressors, this unit dances on hard surfaces — place it on a piece of soft carpet to keep it in place.

Model: No. 180-11
From: Badger
Price: $210.00
Type: Oilless diaphragm (1/12 hp)
Size: 8½″ long, 5″ wide, 7″ high
Weight: 11 lbs.
Air pressure: 34 psi static, 23 psi load
Noise level: Moderate rattle
Features: Automatic shutoff, handle, one-year warranty

Similar to the 180-1, this unit has an added automatic shutoff — the machine stops operating when you stop airbrushing. The pressure level of the auto shutoff feature is adjustable.

Model: No. 34-2025
From: Binks Manufacturing Co., 9201 West Belmont Avenue, Franklin Park, IL 60131
Price: $190.00
Type: Oilless diaphragm (1/8 hp)
Size: 8″ long, 6″ wide, 7″ high
Weight: 9 lbs.
Air pressure: 27 psi static, 18 psi load
Noise level: Moderate rattle
Features: One-year warranty

Another oilless diaphragm, but this time it's upside down — the cylinder head serves as the base. Air-hose coupling is also on the base, so attaching the hose is slightly more difficult. Unit will not start against a load — depress airbrush air button before plugging the compressor in.

Model: No. 34-3010 Wob-l Moe Air 2
From: Binks
Price: $325.00
Type: Oilless piston (1/2 hp)
Size: 11″ long, 7″ wide, 12″ high
Weight: 22 lbs.
Air pressure: See below
Noise level: Loud rattle
Features: Switch on body, one-year warranty

The instructions caution that you should attach a bleeder valve before op-erating this compressor with an airbrush, but no bleeder valve was supplied. I used one from another compressor. With the airbrush operating, air escaped from the bleeder valve as well as the relief valve. This unit puts out more air than an airbrush can handle, and without a storage tank I found it unsuitable for airbrushing. I couldn't get a pressure reading with the regulator because the gauge fluctuated wildly under the strain.

Model: No. HS-201 Speedy Sprayer
From: W.R. Brown Co., 901 East 22nd Street, North Chicago, IL 60064
Price: $114.95
Type: Oilless piston
Size: 7″ long, 4″ wide, 5″ high
Weight: 6 lbs.
Air pressure: 22 psi static, 11 psi load
Noise level: Moderate rattle
Features: Tiny; includes bleeder valve, one-year warranty

Similar in design and performance to the Badger 80-1 Whirlwind, the HS-201 is tiny, but at 11 psi there's barely enough pressure to spray thinned hobby paints. Least expensive unit tested.

Model: No. HS-410 Speedy Sprayer
From: W.R. Brown Co.
Price: $155.95
Type: Oilless diaphragm
Size: 9″ long, 5″ wide, 7″ high
Weight: 11 lbs.
Air pressure: 21 psi static, 14 psi load
Noise level: Moderate rattle
Features: Includes bleeder valve, toggle switch on body, one-year warranty

Another typical oilless diaphragm design, the HS-410 has an added toggle switch on the body. This unit, like other diaphragm compressors without automatic shutoff, should always be used with a bleeder valve (included).

Model: No. D-500
From: Paasche Airbrush Co., 7440 West Lawrence Avenue, Harwood Heights, IL 60656
Price: $145.00
Type: Oilless diaphragm (1/10 hp)
Size: 8″ long, 5″ wide, 7″ high
Weight: 12 lbs.
Air pressure: 25 psi static, 18 psi load

Noise level: Moderate rattle
Features: Bleeder valve, one-year warranty

Another typical diaphragm unit, the Paasche D-500 comes with a bleeder valve to prevent pressure buildup. Like most diaphragm units, it is somewhat noisy and dances on hard surfaces.

Model: D
From: Paasche
Price: $225.00
Type: Oilless diaphragm (1/4 hp)
Size: 12″ long, 7″ wide, 11″ high
Weight: 17 lbs.
Air pressure: 28 psi static, 23 psi load
Noise level: Moderate rattle
Features: Domed diaphragm design, line switch, one-year warranty

Paasche's D model is perhaps the old-est design we tested. The domed diaphragm section appears unchanged through many years in the Paasche catalog, but this unit comes with a larger, more modern motor casing. A convenient handle is installed over a long pipe fitting at the air outlet. The D model is more powerful than the other diaphragm units we tested, providing 23 psi while spraying. The line switch is convenient.

COMPRESSORS WITH STORAGE TANKS

Model: No. HS-375
From: W.R. Brown Co.
Price: $459.95
Type: Oilless diaphragm (1/3 hp) with 5-gallon storage tank
Size: 20″ long, 9″ wide, 18″ high
Weight: 38 lbs.
Air pressure: Sustains up to 30 psi
Noise level: Loud rattle

Perhaps the second most popular design, this is the next step up from a standard diaphragm unit. The unit is noisy when running, but not as loud as the Campbell Hausfeld compressors.

Sustained pressure of 30 psi should cover most airbrushing needs. The compressor kicks on after 75 seconds of spraying at 30 psi, and takes 20 seconds to fill. Air hissing at the end of the charge cycle is normal. The air outlet shutoff valve is convenient — when you stop airbrushing, closing the valve will keep air leaks from triggering the compressor to charge the tank.

Model: No. MT-5012 Power Pal
From: Campbell Hausfeld, Production Drive, Harrison, OH 45030-1477
Price: $179.99
Type: Oilless piston (½ hp) with storage tank
Size: 19″ long, 10″ wide, 22″ high

Weight: 39 lbs.
Air pressure: See comments
Noise level: Loud rattle
Features: "Regulator," tank pressure gauge, detachable tank (see below), 15′ air hose, one-year warranty

This is a typical household compressor designed for light air tools, spray guns, and filling inflatables, but with unusual features. The MT-5012 allows you to use the compressor alone, with the 6-gallon storage tank, or the tank alone. The compressor attaches to a bracket on the tank with two hex nuts, the air outlet to the tank with a rubber hose. A gauge tells you the pressure in the tank, but without an additional regulator there's no way to control the line pressure from the tank.

The compressor has a "regulator," but this is actually a simple variable bleeder valve — if you need 30 psi from the compressor, you dial it with the regulator knob and the excess air is dumped through the bleeder.

Filling the tank requires your attention — there is no automatic shutoff, but a safety valve is installed. I filled the tank to its maximum pressure (about 100 psi) and with the regulator/filter (not included) attached to the outlet I was able to spray at 30 psi for about 5 minutes. When the tank pressure drops below the desired pressure, you have to switch on the compressor to recharge.

Look for Campbell Hausfeld compressors at hardware stores and home-improvement centers.

Model: No. MT-500102 AJ Power Pal
From: Campbell Hausfeld

Price: $229.00
Type: Oilless piston (¾ hp) with storage tank
Size: 22″ long, 14″ wide, 20″ high (without handle)
Weight: 48 lbs.
Air pressure: Sustains up to 90 psi
Noise level: Loud rattle
Features: 7½-gallon tank, tank pressure dial and line pressure regulator, 15′ air hose, moisture drain, wheels, handle, one-year warranty

Similar to the MT-5012, this unit is more powerful and is permanently attached to its 7½-gallon storage tank.

Unlike the MT-5012, the MT-5001 has an automatic shutoff and automatically kicks on to fill the tank when the pressure drops. Two gauges show the tank pressure and the outlet line pressure. The ¾-horsepower, two-cylinder compressor is powerful enough to run small air tools and spray guns. The wheels and handle make it easy to move about, but like the MT-5012, this compressor is LOUD! I was able to spray for 127 seconds at 30 psi, then the unit kicked in and recharged the tank in 40 seconds.

SILENT COMPRESSORS

Model: No. 34-1181
From: Binks
Price: $450.00
Type: Silent (⅙ hp)
Size: 15″ long, 7″ wide, 11″ high
Weight: 34 lbs.
Air pressure: Sustains up to 30 psi
Noise level: Low hum
Features: Regulator/filter, switch, handle, one-year warranty

An encased, refrigerator-type silent compressor similar to the Air Pro 1. The unit provided air for 9 seconds at 30 psi before recharging and took 14 seconds to fill. I found the instructions confusing since they show a generic silent compressor. Made in Italy.

Model: No. 34-1183
From: Binks
Price: $565.00
Type: Silent (⅓ hp)
Size: 15″ long, 7″ wide, 18″ high
Weight: 34 lbs.
Air pressure: Sustains up to 50 psi
Noise level: Low hum
Features: Regulator/filter, switch, tubular handle, one-year warranty

This silent compressor is arranged vertically and (although taller) uses less floor space than the comparable AMI or Jun-Air. It provided air for 17 seconds at 30 psi, then took 15 seconds to fill. Made in Italy.

Model: Minor No. 3
From: Jun-Air Inc., 1303 Barclay Blvd., Buffalo Grove, IL 60089
Price: $455.00
Type: Silent
Size: 12″ long, 18″ wide, 12″ high
Weight: 33 lbs.
Air pressure: Sustains up to 40 psi
Noise level: Low hum
Features: Open design, regulator, no switch, tubular handle, one-year warranty

The Jun-Air is a refrigerator-style compressor similar to the AMI unit. The side-by-side construction allows it to fit under a shelf. Unlike the other silent machines we tested, this one has no switch, but a green power light lets you know it is running. The Jun-Air Minor provided 12 seconds of air at 30 psi before the unit kicked on and filled the tank in 12 seconds. Made in Denmark.

Recommendations: The Badger 80-2 Whirlwind and W.R. Brown HS-201 work fine for spraying inks and low-viscosity paints, but I feel they are underpowered for airbrushing most hobby paints. All the diaphragm units provide enough air pressure for hobby paints. Automatic shutoffs and switches are worthwhile features. I found the Binks Moe-Air 2 to be too powerful for airbrushing — it puts out more air than the airbrush can handle.

All the silent, refrigerator-style compressors work well, and they really are quiet. But silence is golden, and you pay the price.

The household compressors from Campell Hausfield will work with airbrushes and can be useful for many other chores. However, they are noisy, so be prepared for the racket.

Whichever compressor you choose, read the instructions carefully and don't abuse the machine. It may be the most expensive modeling tool you own. With care, it should last a lifetime.

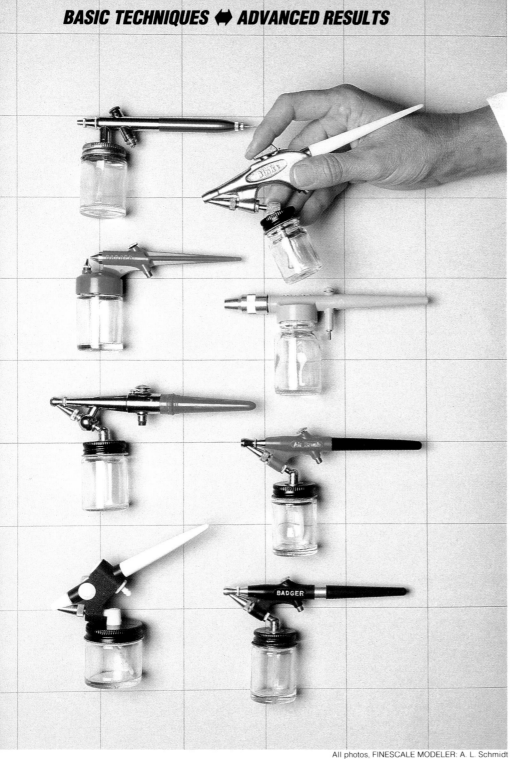

All photos, FINESCALE MODELER: A. L. Schmidt

Single-action airbrushes are inexpensive and ideal for painting models. (Left column from top) Badger 200, Badger, 250, Paasche H, HS831. (Right from top) Binks Wren, X-acto Magic Touch (no longer made), Polk 8114, Badger 350.

Basic airbrushes for basic airbrushing

A survey of seven single-action airbrushes — including how to use them

Fig. 1. Propellant cans are the cheapest way to start airbrushing, but only last about 30 minutes. A can costs about $5.00. The can and valve assembly come with some airbrush sets.

Fig. 2. The most popular method of providing air for the airbrush is a compressor. Simple diaphragm units like this one sell for around $100.00.

BY PAUL BOYER

THE AIRBRUSH IS, to many modelers, the *only* way to paint models. To some, the airbrush is the badge of the professional or *serious* modeler — true, most pros and contest winners paint with an airbrush, but if you're a beginner, you might want an airbrush to make painting models easier, and help them look better.

An airbrush is a miniature spray gun that mixes paint and air into a fine mist. It's perfect for applying color in small areas or for producing intricate camouflage patterns.

An investment. Getting started in airbrushing is going to cost money, but

Fig. 4. Cylinders of compressed or liquified air or CO_2 provide a quiet air source, ideal for apartment dwellers. This rig costs $150.00; a refill costs $6.00.

Fig. 3. Compressors with holding tanks are quieter because the compressor only operates when the tank's pressure drops. They also provide a steady airflow to the airbrush. This unit costs $300.00.

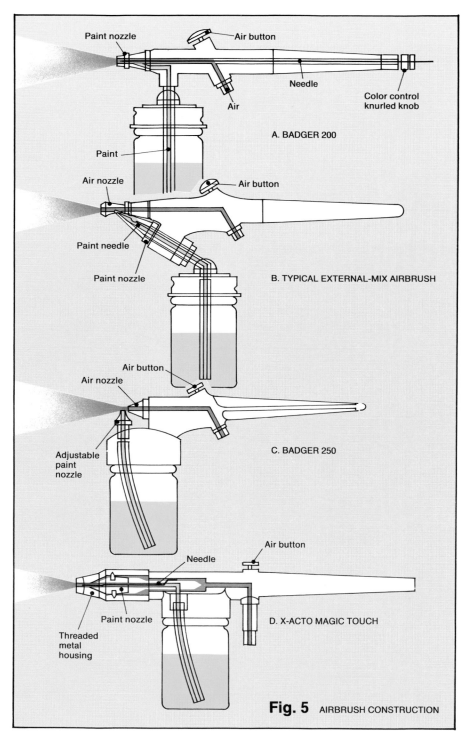

Paint nozzle — Air button — Needle — Color control knurled knob — Paint — Air

A. BADGER 200

Air nozzle — Air button — Paint needle — Paint nozzle

B. TYPICAL EXTERNAL-MIX AIRBRUSH

Air button — Air nozzle — Adjustable paint nozzle

C. BADGER 250

Air button — Needle — Paint nozzle — Threaded metal housing

D. X-ACTO MAGIC TOUCH

Fig. 5 AIRBRUSH CONSTRUCTION

your investment will be in equipment that should last for years of modeling. Most single-action airbrushes cost under $50.00, including air hose, paint bottle, and sometimes a small can of compressed gas (propellant). Many manufacturers offer airbrush sets with more bottles and accessories, so read the literature at your hobby shop.

If you only plan to airbrush occasionally, a propellant can is adequate, Fig. 1; it costs around $5.00 and holds enough propellant to paint for about 30 minutes. If you plan to do a lot of airbrushing, you'll want to look at a more economical air supply.

Air compressors, Fig. 2, are the usual choice. These electrically driven units

come in a variety of sizes and cost between $100.00 and $300.00. The more expensive units have holding tanks, Fig. 3, eliminating the pulsating pressure from simple diaphragm compressors. They are also quieter — the compressor kicks on only when the air pressure in the tank falls below a certain level, builds up the pressure again, then shuts off automatically.

For the ultimate in quiet operation, consider a cylinder of compressed air or carbon dioxide (CO_2), Fig. 4. You can purchase a 20-pound cylinder and regulator for about $150.00, or they can be

leased from compressed gas supply companies. The biggest drawback is that the gas will eventually run out and you'll have to haul it to a supplier for a refill (a 20-pound refill of compressed CO_2 costs around $6.00).

The single-action airbrush. For most modelers, the single-action airbrush is adequate, and many consider it ideal. The term single action is a bit misleading — it means that the button controls only the airflow, on or off. The paint flow is controlled by a separate adjustable needle or color control, usually at the front of the airbrush. Turn-

Badger Airbrush Co.
9128 W. Belmont Ave.
Franklin Park, IL 60131
BADGER 250
Basic set (250-1) $25.00
Includes: 6' hose, 2 ¾-oz bottles
Minimum spray pattern: ¼"
Maximum spray pattern: 1"
Good for one-color and masked subjects.

Badger Airbrush Co.
9128 W. Belmont Ave.
Franklin Park, IL 60131
BADGER 350
Basic set (350-1) $38.00
Includes: 2-oz bottle, ¾-oz bottle (no hose)
Minimum spray pattern: ³⁄₃₂"
Maximum spray pattern: ½"
Basic external-mix design.

W.R. Brown Co.
901 E. 22nd Street
North Chicago, IL 60064
INTERMATIC
Basic set (HS831) $41.50
Includes: 1-oz bottle, 6' hose
Minimum spray pattern: ¹⁄₁₆"
Maximum spray pattern: ⅝"
Mostly plastic. Has air volume adjust knob. Bleeder button provided.

Paasche Airbrush Co.
7440 W. Lawrence Ave.
Harwood Heights, IL 60656
PAASCHE H1
Complete set $38.00
Includes: ¼-oz cup, 3-oz bottle, tools, hanger, booklet (no hose)
Minimum spray pattern: ¹⁄₁₆"
Maximum spray pattern: ½"
Oldest design tested. Mostly metal. Has air volume adjust knob.

ing the nozzle counterclockwise opens the valve and allows more paint to be drawn up by the air blowing across the tip. So there are *two* controls on a *single-action* airbrush.

On the other hand, the button on a double-action airbrush controls the airflow (push down) and the paint flow (rocking the button pulls the needle back and opens the tip). Double-action airbrushes usually cost between $60.00 and $100.00, which puts them beyond the scope of this article.

Internal and external mix. Most single-action airbrushes are external-mix designs — the air and paint mix outside the body of the airbrush. Figure 5b shows a cross section of a typical single-action, external-mix airbrush — the Badger 350, Binks Wren, Intermatic, Paasche H, and Polk are similar. The Badger 200 and X-acto Magic Touch are internal-mix units. The air is routed through the air valve and around the front of a longitudinal needle where the air stream siphons the paint from the bottle and mixes with it.

Testing airbrushes. I rounded up eight single-action airbrushes usually found in hobby shops and mail-order houses. The old standby Badger, Binks, and Paasche airbrushes are probably the most familiar to modelers, and re-

placement parts and accessories can be found alongside them in many hobby shops and art supply stores.

I tested each airbrush by spraying Gunze Sangyo Aqueous Hobby color diluted two parts paint to one part thinner (a 50/50 mix of isopropyl alcohol and water with a drop of liquid dishwashing detergent to cut surface tension). Each airbrush was hooked up to the compressed air line in the FSM workshop and the regulator was set for 25 psi (pounds per square inch) pressure. I adjusted the color control of each until I got the thinnest sustainable line (usually with the tip held ½" from the sheet styrene test surface). Then I

Badger Airbrush Co.
9128 W. Belmont Ave.
Franklin Park, IL 60131

BADGER 200
Basic set (200-1) $55.00

Includes: 2 ¾-oz bottles (no hose)
Minimum spray pattern: 1/16″
Maximum spray pattern: 1/2″
Internal-mix design similar to double-action airbrushes.

Binks Manufacturing Co.
9201 W. Belmont Ave.
Franklin Park, IL 60131

BINKS WREN
Basic set (59-10003) $68.75

Includes: ½-oz bottle (no hose)
Minimum spray pattern: 1/16″
Maximum spray pattern: 5/8″
Most comfortable tested. Has air volume adjust knob. Permanent air nozzle.

Polk's Model Craft Hobbies, Inc.
314 Fifth Ave. New York, NY 10001

POLK'S
Basic set (8114) $24.95

Includes: ¾-oz bottle, 2-oz bottle, 6′ hose, propellant, valve, tool
Minimum spray pattern: 3/32″
Maximum spray pattern: 1/2″
Made in Taiwan, similar in appearance to Badger 350. Not recommended due to design and manufacturing defects (see text)

opened the valve for the maximum line, sprayed from about 3″ away. I disassembled the color control of each airbrush and cleaned it, looking for problems and defects.

The summaries on this two-page spread list the specifics for each airbrush and my test results. Prices are for the least expensive airbrush set; more expensive sets include more accessories.

The Badger 250. The simplest of all the airbrushes I tested, the Badger 250

should more properly be called a miniature spray gun. The unit is mostly plastic with a simple metal paint nozzle that meets the airflow at a 90-degree angle, Fig. 5c. The spray pattern goes from 1/4″ to 1″, fine for painting one-color subjects.

The Badger 350. This is the only Badger of the three I tested that is of typical single-action airbrush design. The color control is the classic needle valve that meets the airflow at roughly

a 45-degree angle. The body of the 350 is plastic, but the color control and air tip are metal. It's available with fine, medium, and heavy tips. With the fine tip the 350 sprays down to 3/32″ and opens to 1/2″.

The Badger 200. The shape of the all-metal Badger 200 is similar to a double-action airbrush, but it lacks the one-button air-and-color control. Figure 5a is a cross section of the Badger 200, a single-action internal-mix airbrush, combining simple controls of the single-action with the linear construction of the internal-mix airbrush. The amount of paint sprayed is controlled by turning the knurled knob at the rear of the body which moves the needle in and out. I was able to obtain a 1/16″ steady line with the IL (medium) tip; opened up, I got a 1/2″ pattern.

Disassembling the airbrush isn't difficult, but the 200 requires the most care when cleaning. The thin, sharp needle and fragile paint nozzle can be easily damaged.

The Binks Wren. The Wren has served modelers virtually unchanged for close to 25 years. The streamlined metal body with the finger-fitting air release button is the most comfortable of all the airbrushes I tested. The Wren has a setscrew that allows some adjustment of the air volume by limiting the depression of the button.

The paint tip screws into the body of the Wren, the most precise method of alignment of all the external-mix, single-action airbrushes I tested. The air nozzle is not interchangeable — the Wren B I tested has a medium (B) air tip, but I substituted a fine (A) paint nozzle for the medium and the combination worked well, producing a $1/16''$ line and a $1/2''$ line wide open.

The W.R. Brown HS831. Although based on the typical single-action design, the Intermatic has a couple of new wrinkles. The body, air nozzle, air button, and air hose fitting are plastic. The metal color control is held in the body with a spring-loaded ball bearing; the entire control can pass through the mounting hole. However, when a fully loaded paint bottle is attached, this fitting sometimes gives way under the weight and allows the entire paint line to slip out of the body.

A knurled knob on the side of the body allows some adjustment of the air pressure — I found this stiff and difficult to use. The unit comes with two air buttons, one designed to be used with piston-type compressors to allow the air to bleed off through the button; the other button doesn't bleed air. When I hooked up the airbrush to the air line, a little air was coming out of the air nozzle before I depressed the button — perhaps there is a part missing in the air valve assembly. With the fine tip, the HS831 produced a $1/16''$ line and opened to $5/8''$.

The Paasche H. Although the oldest design of all the airbrushes I tested, the trusty H model remains an industry standard. The main portion of the body is metal with a plastic handle. The interchangeable tip is held in place with an Allen-head setscrew. The air release button is well back on the body — the H is not the most comfortable airbrush to operate. With the No. 1 tip (finest), I could get down to $1/16''$, and wide open to $1/2''$. This model also has an air control setscrew which allows some variance of air volume by limiting how far down the button is pressed. I didn't test Paasche's model F, a smaller version of the H.

Polk's 8114. This airbrush is made in Taiwan and is a lot like the Badger 350. It comes with a fine tip, but no larger tips are available.

This airbrush had three defects, two in design and one in manufacturing. The thread on the paint tip is designed to hold the paint nozzle and the locknut, but there isn't enough thread to allow the locknut to hold the tip tight to the body of the airbrush. I had to force the locknut partially beyond the threads with small pliers. Inside the paint nozzle is a plastic compression washer that keeps paint from dripping out of the nozzle. The retaining nut that threads inside didn't have a slot, making it extremely difficult to remove for cleaning or replacing the washer. The third problem I had was with the siphon bottle cap — the coupling's solder joint came apart, leaving a portion in the airbrush while the bottle fell away (and creating a mess). Once I got it to operate, Polk's airbrush gave a minimum spray of $3/32''$ and opened to $1/2''$.

Using a basic airbrush. Getting the most out of any airbrush takes experimentation and lots of practice, and you may obtain better (or worse) results than I did in the tests. You should get good performance from the Badger 350, the internal-mix Badger 200, the binks Wren, and the Paasche H. The W.R. Brown HS831 will give good results, once you get used to its unusual design features, but the Polk single-action's troubles can't be ignored — pass this one by. The Badger 250 can't perform like the others, but it's adequate for painting one-color subjects.

Whatever your choice, be sure to practice a lot! Your first efforts probably won't look anything like what you expect, but in time you'll understand the idiosyncracies of your airbrush. Experiment with paints, thinning ratios and various air pressures to see what works best for you. Keep the airbrush clean and inspect the color control and air nozzle occasionally. Again, the key to successful airbrushing is practice, practice, practice.

PAINTING AND FINISHING SCALE MODELS

SCALE MODELING HANDBOOK NO. 10

BY PAUL BOYER

FineScale MODELER

Continuity: Michael Emmerich
Art Director: Lawrence Luser
Artists: Lisa Bergman
Phil Kirchmeier

KALMBACH BOOKS

First printing, 1991. Second printing, 1992.

The material in this book first appeared
as articles in FINESCALE MODELER magazine
They are reprinted here in their entirety.

Getting from here to there. For some, a kit out of the box is a tantalizing project in the rough. For others, it's a daunting experiment with fears of botched paint jobs, tangled decals, and an overall poor replica clouding the dream of a well-finished model. FSM's Finishing School will help you through all stages of painting and finishing your models.

FSM'S FINISHING SCHOOL

THE THRILL IS GONE. Your two most recent kits lie unfinished, gathering dust. Your problems seem insurmountable: Trouble with painting, decaling, or weathering leads to frustration, and frustration leads to putting the model aside.

Even worse, anticipating similar problems for the next project may prevent you from starting. Your dreams of display cases full of attractive models to show to your friends, children, and grandchildren evaporate. You even consider taking up golf — now *that's* frustration!

But help is on the way. You enroll in *FineScale Modeler's* Finishing School, where the faculty promises to help you overcome your finishing frustrations.

The course work won't be easy, and you'll have to pay attention, but it's a correspondence course, and you can proceed at your own pace.

The purpose of FSM's Finishing School is not to make you a prizewinning modeler, but a competent, confident, and contented modeler. The course will concentrate on finishes — paints, decals, and the final touches in creating attractive models. Advanced topics like superdetailing, conversions, customizing, or scratchbuilding won't be discussed — the goal is to show you techniques to produce good-looking models without a lot of work and worry. Once you've mastered these skills, you'll be able to complete every model, every time, and enjoy the hobby more, too.